Ancient England

1. THE EASTERN CHAPEL, FOUNTAINS ABBEY, YORKSHIRE, BEFORE TREATMENT

From a coloured lithograph by William Richardson, ca. 1845

Ancient England

A REVIEW OF MONUMENTS AND REMAINS IN PUBLIC CARE AND OWNERSHIP

By

EDMUND VALE

Illustrated by Photographs and Drawings

LONDON
B. T. BATSFORD LTD.
15 NORTH AUDLEY STREET, W.1
& MALVERN WELLS, WORCESTERSHIRE

First published Winter 1941

TO

WILFRID HEMP, F.S.A.

W. J. H. I value it that even by such a poor ruse as a dedication I should be able to associate your name with the
contents of this book. Had it been where mine is, as author,
the public would have had a better bargain. But then, you
never would have written a book of this sort. You are an
honest-to-God producer and this is merely "popular" book-
work—a middleman's job.

Archaeologists fulfil a peculiar role in the economy of
public happiness, especially in our times. It is their labours
which provide the office-bound man with some of his chief
delights and refreshments of mentality when he is on holiday,
by presenting him with a key to the romance of the past.
Yet this work is so disinterested that neither the man nor his
achievements are heralded by the fanfares of publicity. So
I feel I must take this opportunity of reminding the sightseer
of some of the things you did for him even before you
crossed the road from H.M. Office of Works to Sanctuary
Buildings to become Secretary of the Royal Commission
on Ancient Monuments for Wales and Monmouthshire.
When the much visited castles of Harlech, Beaumaris, and
Denbigh, and the less frequented ones of Flint and Ewloe
were put into a state of preservation for the Nation you
undertook the historical "side," and were in sole charge of
the difficult and complex reconstruction of those two vastly
interesting prehistoric burial-chambers at Bryn Celli Ddu
and Capel Garmon. The guides to these monuments are
from your pen and are among the most attractive as well as
engrossing of that famous series.

Easter, 1941

MADE AND PRINTED IN GREAT BRITAIN
FOR THE PUBLISHERS, B. T. BATSFORD LTD., LONDON
BY JARROLD AND SONS LTD., NORWICH

Postscript, 1941

I WOULD explain that this is a 1939 manuscript and is therefore redolent of the peace-time atmosphere. It has not been altered, even to substitute "Ministry" for "Office" of Works. Chapters VI (Monasteries) and VII (Houses) have separate histories. Mr. Batsford found my treatment of both these themes too brief for what he wanted to express in illustration. For the monasteries he preferred to use an older essay of mine, more explicit (if rather heavy-going) and in a more leisurely tempo. As to the chapter on houses, I persuaded him to undertake the amplification of it himself, and he kindly consented to do so. This explains how it is that a solitary chapter bears the name of a second author. What a triumph of co-operation between author and publisher—or is it *toleration* we ought both to get good marks for?

It will seem to many people a little odd and superfluous that just at this time a publisher should chose to bring out a book on old ruins when new ones are being made for us daily. You may think that the reason is not far to seek, namely, that the Publisher, having got the manuscript on hand, and perhaps having paid a weighty sum "in advance on royalties," thought he must make the best of a bad bargain. But that, I am told, is not the case.

The book may prove to have two missions. One, that it is a record of a great achievement consummated in those twenty years of peace-but-not-plenty which were marked by a series of slumps, disappointments, and fruitless political "talks," though by few great deeds of lasting value to humanity, and it is a record which cannot be repeated, be an author never so competent; as it is sadly certain that many of the old buildings described and photographed will be either not there at all when peace comes or only remain in a fragmentary state.

This reason leads to another. If our wealth of ancient monuments is becoming less, it is at the same time becoming more precious, and many people who have given no more than a tourist's casual thought to those "old world sights" (that they took for granted would be there to look at again on the next holiday) may be stirred to deeper reflections on them. In this case a well illustrated book may serve as magic-carpet transport when petrol and other means fail.

v

So much, then, in support of the argument for publishing the book during the *Blitz*! It was not, anyhow, my concern. All the same, I admire Mr. Batsford's courage and, for my part, I hope that the tourist, now turned combatant, will feel more than ever convinced when he has read the book that he is fighting for a heritage in spirit as well as in land that is worth while.

I have been a diligent pilgrim to the shrines whereof I write, not for the mere sake of enjoying the expeditions (though, God knows, I have enjoyed every minute) or getting "copy," in the journalese sense, but in a desperate attempt to understand the story in stone as a whole, together with its application to our present mode of life, and with its bearings on the future. These fragments show a man something more than the written word of history and romance, because they are not a convention but reality. And they are seldom wrought after the image of a single mind, but represent the mentality of a people and of a period of culture or anti-culture. Each one of itself may have a peculiarity or a beauty or a clue to this or that, a clue which gives a lead to the imagination—where the dictionary is still too limited to help. But each one is only a part of the whole, and it is the whole that must be grappled with if we are to get an inkling as to the meaning of the story of the English people. It is a strange, complex story, not by any means concerned with the coming of the Anglo-Saxon or any one race to these islands. For, if you know your clues, you can trace the prejudice of the Stone Age right down to our own time.

During that score of years between this war and the last it was being said by many of ourselves as well as foreigners that the story of the English people was not worth hearing. But those people did not know what the story really was. How could they? It is not a thing that can be picked up from scraps of school history or, indeed, from any history book. History amplifies and annotates. But the solid text of the story is in fashioned masonry. And this speaks not only to the mind but to the heart because of its actual contacts with the men long gone who made us what we are.

Now the night sky is full of the noise of a fierce and

vindictive enemy bent on destroying us, and this challenge has re-awakened our faith in the culture we stood for. But perhaps it is not too much to say that if we had understood how to look back we should not have been caught off our guard and this hideous thing would never have happened.

3, The Green, Llandaff   E. V.
Spring 1941

Acknowledgment

THE Publishers must acknowledge their obligation to the following photographers, whose work appears in the illustrations: the late Major Allen (collection now in the possession of the Ashmolean Museum, Oxford), figs 16, 22, 37; The British Council, for work by J. Dixon Scott, f.r.p.s., figs. 21, 55, 61, 78, 81, 94, 96; the late Brian C. Clayton, figs. 14, 17, 20, 30, 32, 34, 35, 36, 38, 39, 40, 41, 42, 43, 44, 45, 46, 47, 50, 53, 57, 58, 65, 66, 74, 75, 80, 83, 84, 86, 91, 92, 93, 95, 99; Mr. Herbert Felton, f.r.p.s., figs. 2, 3, 24, 48, 49, 51, 69, 76, 77, 100, 109, 118; Mr. R. C. Gardner, fig. 29; Mr. L. Gayton, figs. 27, 87; Mr. F. A. Girling, fig. 52; The Ministry of Works and Buildings, figs. 4, 5, 6, 11, 12, 33, 59; Mr. A. W. Hutton, fig. 54; Mr. A. F. Kersting, fig. 120; the Mustograph Agency, Ltd., figs. 10, 15, 19, 60, 67, 70, 101, 110; Mr. Will F. Taylor, figs. 7, 8, 9, 23, 25, 26, 28, 56, 62, 63, 64, 68, 71, 72, 79, 85, 88, 97, 102, 103, 108, 119; Miss M. Wight, figs. 13, 37a, 82; Mr. F. R. Winstone, f.r.p.s., figs. 18, 73, 90, 98.

The frontispiece is from a coloured lithograph by W. Richardson, and fig. 114 is from a watercolour by Leonard Squirrell, R.I., by kind permission of Messrs. Cowell, Ltd., of Ipswich, who have printed the plate. The plan of the Cashtel-yn-Ard Barrow on p. 18 is by Mr. Grahame Clark, f.s.a., in his *Prehistory of the Isle of Man*, the plan of the Chambered Cairn, Goward, co. Down is by permission of the Belfast Naturalists Field Club, and the Celtic brooch on p. 30, drawn by Ruth Vale, is from *How to See England*, by the Author, by kind permission of Messrs. Methuen & Co., Ltd. The drawings on pp. 15 and 20 are by Marjorie Quennell from *Everyday Life in the New Stone, Bronze, and Early Iron Ages*; that on p. 102 is from Prior's *Gothic Art in England*, by permission of Messrs. George Bell & Sons, Ltd., and that on p. 145 is by Mr. W. Curtis Green, r.a., f.r.i.b.a. Fig. 131 is by his kind permission from a drawing by Professor E. W. Tristram, f.s.a.

Contents

2 The spurred towers, Goodrich Castle, Herefordshire

3   The Courtyard, Goodrich Castle, cleared by the Office of Works

CHAPTER I

Ruination

THE hard-headed tell us that "you cannot get away from facts"; by which they mean that they do not admit the existence in life of mystery and illusion. Perhaps I am wrong, but it has always seemed to me that for every matter of fact there is a matter of mystery to balance it, and if one age produces an infallible Newton the next will produce an infallible Einstein to confute him. The generation of our immediate predecessors took a pride in the exaltation of God and men, in making heroes and worshipping them, in creating a façade: whereas the men of our age take delight in smashing every detail of that façade and debunking the authors of it.

In the midst of this orgy of iconoclasm it is not a little surprising to find that relics of the past are receiving more attention than in any previous age and that ruined buildings and the less articulate works of prehistory have become the special care of the State, which now spends large sums annually in nursing them. That the romantics should ruin their ruins, and the debunkers preserve them, sounds paradoxical. But there is a consistent point of view, for the preservation of a ruin often (if not always) offers the supreme opportunity for debunking it.

THE PROGRESSIVE RUIN

It is important at this stage to find a proper answer to the question "What is the good of a ruin?" And in order to do that it must be realized that there are two sorts of ruins, and that the Victorians preferred one kind and ourselves the other. The hall of the lord which becomes a tenement dwelling of the poor, then a hen-roost, then a pigstye, and finally a roofless derelict is an object in which decay and the vicissitudes of evolution are continually active—it

2   I

moves slowly but surely from somethingness to nothingness, and may therefore be called a *progressive* ruin.

But if at some stage in its process of vanishing such a ruin has its normal development arrested by an act of preservation (calculated to make it unalterable) and has a fixed standard of tidiness imposed on it (calculated to remain constant) it will become a *static* ruin, which is something quite different from the first kind. So the "good of a ruin" may be that it rouses the imagination of the beholder, either constructively or creatively. And a roused imagination is a fine thing for any man to have.

The progressive ruin is rapidly becoming a thing of the past. Stonehenge is bedded in concrete and Tintern Abbey has its pillars rebuilt round steel cores (4, 5). But a few are still to be seen, such as the castles of Okehampton and Llanstephan, Wenlock and Lilleshall Abbeys. And a few are in a transitional stage wherein decay has been partially arrested without the tidying-up standard having been imposed, such as Conway Castle (54) and Fountains Abbey (1, 80, 83, 84). All these buildings are now worth visiting, not only because they are ruins but because they are *real* ruins of the old style.

What the Victorian expected to get out of his ruin was not exact knowledge but "atmosphere" and "improvement," vague terms in themselves but, as intellectual goals for an expedition, singularly parallel to those of an earlier generation which went on pilgrimage to the shrines of the saints. Where the pilgrims performed mysteries before their shrines the Victorians ate sandwiches. And where the Victorians ate sandwiches we take snapshots. The pilgrim believed that his reward was to be put into touch with the efficacy of the saint, the Victorian believed that his reward was to be put into touch with the romance of the situation. But it is almost too soon to say what we ourselves believe in when we visit our preserved ruins. The cult is a new one and its priesthood is puritanically inclined, so far as mysteries are concerned. In fact, as I have hinted, we owe it to the present fashion of debunking that so much care is being bestowed on our "ancient monuments." In exorcising

2

druids, ghosts, dungeons, blood-stains, bats, and ivy, the scientific archaeologists of our prosaic time have been able to adapt our revolutionary principle to suit their own ends better than any other cultural body. Thus, they have undoubtedly saved for us and for posterity those very relics and altars that have provoked veneration in the past and it is for us to find the new imaginative formula of approach.

THE STATIC RUIN

When the ruin that was neglected and let go is put into a state of preservation and tidied up we do actually lose something that is irreplaceable, and that is the vivid presentment of the ravage of Time. We may also lose certain artistic values which used to belong to the ruin when it formed the keynote of a wild setting, or when it made a striking note of contrast, as when a thatched, whitewashed labourer's cottage was seen to make use of the curtain of a vast fortress for its back wall.

But it is quite clear that only this and perhaps the next generation could have gone on enjoying these fruits of decay. The third generation would have had no ruined mediaeval buildings to look at, with or without ivy. However, that is not the only gain. In most cases where preservative treatment has been applied excavation has also gone on (13). By this means the Prehistoric period has been illuminated beyond the wildest hopes of the older generation of antiquaries and historians, the story of the Roman occupation of Britain has been changed from a bare outline to a profound volume, in which not only events but innumerable named personalities have their place; and even the comparatively well-documented history of the Mediaeval period has had new chapters added to it. So, whereas the old cult of ruins was based on fiction, the new is based on fact, hard fact! But if you agreed with what I said in my first paragraph you must hold with me that for every fact there is a mystery. Even the mathematicians make use of mysteries by adopting symbols for them and the most practical symbol for a historical mystery is none other than a home-made fiction. By this argument I hope to impress you with the idea that, while the archaeologist is allowed to establish the facts which "you cannot get away from," the layman who goes to see his preserved ancient monuments is at liberty to make his own fictions to offset them. By that team-work the glamour of our antiquities, although re-orientated, will not only be permanently established but greatly enhanced.

This great movement of saving the mute witnesses of our past for the edification of our grandchildren has had its origin within the present century, and has been pushed forward with amazing enthusiasm and unselfish zeal by pioneers of the new technique. Yet the public and the Press have remained quite apathetic. Perhaps it is that they do not realise the far-reaching implications of the enterprise. Or perhaps it is the deadening influence of that awful modern hobgoblin called the School Certificate, which poisons the minds of the young against anything which, in later life, appears to them in the light of a school subject. At any rate the work is going forward with all the original impetus of the enthusiasts still unchecked; but it is really high time that the public took a more lively interest, if only to constitute an active oracle of criticism, for with the best will in the world all enthusiasts are apt to overdo things if not watched.

PRESERVATION

The first public preserver was the National Trust, which was incorporated by Act of Parliament in 1907, having been then in existence as a private body for twelve years. In 1913 the Ancient Monuments Act was passed, whereby the State admitted a cultural responsibility towards its own history never before assumed by the British government. With characteristic thoroughness it created a special department within its own organisation for the scheduling, supervision, and when necessary, the maintenance of all those relics which the makers of our history had left behind them. The new Department of Ancient Monuments was created within the already existing framework of His Majesty's Office of Works.[1]

[1] Now (1941) raised to the dignity of a Ministry.

These two bodies are to-day the principal conservators of our ancient monuments, though not the only ones. But the responsibilities which they accept are different in kind, and their attitudes towards the objects of their care, their points of view, and ways of doing things are sufficiently divergent to provide an interesting contrast. Without overlapping, they often lend support to each other, as when the Office of Works protects the fabric of Stonehenge and the National Trust preserves its solitude.

The Ancient Monuments Department of His Majesty's Office of Works, now the Ministry of Works, does not accept technical ownership of a building as the National Trust does;—it only undertakes the guardianship of it, having made such arrangements with the owner as to insure that its work will not be interfered with, and that it will not be expelled from the premises during its term of guardianship.

The Department was no sooner created than the Great War broke out, and it was not until 1919 that it was able to set to work in earnest. It is now therefore beyond the end of its second effective decade. During that time it has made great growth in organisation and in the scope of its activities. But the most important feature of its growth has been that of its own education in methods of preservation. In this it had to start almost from the beginning and face the most diverse and exacting problems, such as how to stop dry-rot, to scotch the death-watch beetle, to shore up the whole side of a castle about to fall over the edge of a precipice through a perverse streak of geology, how to reinforce crumbling walls, tottering arcades, and crazy window tracery, without these measures being detected by the eye of the sightseer. None of these lessons could be learned from any other sources except its own ingenuity. It may be blamed for a few failures within our own time, but its successes can never be hailed with praise within its own hearing, for they have been aimed with poetical boldness to mature in centuries far, far off. There is an element of romance in that alone, that the visitor to the "treated" ruin should be mindful of.

TREATMENT

When a ruin is offered to the Department, it is inspected and reported on. A survey is made and, if the relic is thought worthy of preservation, it is taken in hand. The Chief Inspector of Ancient Monuments and the architect who will take charge of operations then visit the site and decide on the nature and extent of the work then to be carried out.

Nearly all treatment is of a four-fold character and consists of clearing, excavating, and laying-out the building and its ground with a view to future maintenance. The clearing operation includes the weeding of the walls and the removal of débris from their footings. Sometimes this is too formidable to attempt, as at Helmsley, where, although the huge double moat has been cleared, the pavement of the wide courtyards remains several feet below the well-kept sward. Excavation, proper, goes a good deal further than clearing, and is a very costly business which deceives the eye of those unaccustomed to convert bulk into cartloads. I was particularly impressed by the elusiveness of this factor when I visited Uriconium many years ago, not long after the baths had been exposed. An unsightly mound to one side of the Roman basilica caught my eye, and I asked the resident antiquarian why it had not been taken away. He replied, 'I cannot get a carter to estimate for less than one hundred and fifty pounds for its removal." The successful disposal of such débris is one of the most remarkable achievements of the Department in its excavations. Systems of light railway are employed in which turntables play a large part. Even away from rivers and the sea it is difficult to trace the tips.

The ruined monastery is the biggest loser by clearance and excavation, for there is a sweet melancholy about a green trellis over broken tracery that seems to resanctify a desecrated shrine. But when you apply this treatment to a castle you give it back its moats and the effects produced are sometimes quite surprising.

The clearing and re-flooding of the moat at Beaumaris (7)

gave the castle a new and magical individuality, and the new reflections were certainly a better bargain in romance than the old ivy. At White Castle, too, the restoration of the moat added enormously to the grandeur of that stern entrance. In a way, the replacement of the dry moat is even more impressive than that of the wet moat. Anyone who doubts the power of these as a military obstacle should attempt an assault of the mound at Pickering Castle (9) without the aid of a walking-stick.

Clearance and excavation are, in fact, the only harmless forms of restoration, and some of the exposures gained by these means are tantamount to valuable additions in structure. Outstanding examples of such are the stepped plinths of the keeps of Porchester and Bowes, the spurred towers of Goodrich (2), and the whole of the inner ward of Pevensey Castle with the truly fearsome dungeons discovered under the gatehouse.

Restoration, in the more accepted sense, is only carried out within very narrow limits. Fallen arches and groining are made good where the original form is obvious and can be replaced with the very stones themselves. Much valuable crypt-work is thus saved. This is a notable feature in the treatment of the Bishop's Palace at St. David's (10).

The proper treatment of walls is the most vital necessity in prolonging the life of an old building which has lost its roof, and has to withstand the weather on two extra fronts, namely the inside walls and the tops—the most vulnerable place of all. Sometimes these old shells are held in place more by gravity than mortar, which has often decayed and crumbled so as to be of no more use than dust, though there are cases like the "leaning tower" at Bridgnorth where mortar made in the twelfth century has proved indestructible either by Nature or powerful charges of gunpowder.

The treatment of the crumbling wall is by grouting (6). A hole is poked in a well-chosen joint and the nozzle of a hose inserted. Through this water is first of all pumped to wash out soil and rubbish and then liquid cement is forced in. The art of this operation is to persuade the stream of cement to find its way into all unseen interstices and cavities, leaving no weak spots. As a bad wall will absorb many tons of this dope, the weight of the old wall is immensely increased in proportion to its renewed strength, so that if a weak spot is left between the lower and upper stages, it will be exposed to the danger of a bad collapse through the very agency that was intended to give it everlasting life. Grouting is often a lengthy process and absorbs an unbelievable quantity of material. But the only sign that it has been done is a plug of cement here and there where the nozzle of the hose was inserted.

It should not be forgotten that, even in the ivy-covered and grass-grown ruins which were handed over to the Office of Works, or which still remain unregenerate, much is owed to schemes of preservation carried out during the last century and a half under the influence of the Romantic Revival. The work was generally of the roughest sort and quite out of character with the building. But, without it, we should have lost a great deal that has been spared by this means. Even the railway companies have done their bit. I imagine that by now the whole imposing side of Conway Castle would have fallen if the London and North Western Railway had not secured its foundations. Less interested in motive was that salvage of the groining of the Chapter House at Fountains Abbey by a platform of asphalt installed by the Furness Railway.

It is interesting to compare the older methods with those of the extremely careful and conscientious work of the Department. It is much less trouble to point with cement than with lime mortar, for the former is easy to mix and dries quickly. But the effect of cemented joints is horrible, therefore cement (concrete) in connection with walling is only used in places where the eye does not see.

In some ruins difficult operations of underpinning have been carried out, notably at Fountains Abbey, where the fine arcade of the north transept of the church, which had rested on oak piles in swampy ground for seven hundred years, was found to be in imminent danger of collapse. Much has been done in clamping weak joints and broken

5   Building up the stonework

6   Grouting a wall at Furness Abbey

4   The steel core

4, 5   Reconstruction of a pier at Tintern Abbey with a temporary arch of brick

7 Beaumaris Castle, Anglesey, as re-flooded

8 Pevensey Castle

CASTLE MOATS

fragments together with a malleable non-corrosive material called "delta metal." This technique, admirably applied, may be seen in the Eleanor Cross near Northampton, which is illustrated in Figs. 73 and 74. Occasionally it has been necessary to give a weak pillar a steel core. In this case the pillar has to be taken down and rebuilt after the stones have been made to receive the new element of support. Nearly the whole of the nave arcade of Tintern Abbey has been treated in this way (p. 93, 4, 5). Yet it does not show the least sign of ever having been touched.

Improved access is another feature of treated buildings. In old castles, wherever possible, both wall-walks and turret-tops are made accessible to the public, and that, for most of us, is half the fun of the castle. Formerly the high look-outs could only be reached by venturesome boys, often at considerable risk, for no part of these ruins was so ruinous as the tower stair. This particular means of ascent has somehow managed to acquire for itself three separate dictionary names. It may be called a *well* or *newell* stair, or simply a *vice*. In construction these stairs are built up from a number of stones each cut to the shape of a closed fan. When placed one on the other, step-wise, the outer ends took their place with the stones in the round tower, and the inner ends overlapped so as to form a continuous pillar. This was one of the most ingenious architectural devices of the Middle Ages, but very hard to replace when broken. The Office of Works, however, hit on the idea of rebuilding these well stairs with light units made in concrete instead of stone. This is easily done with a box-mould, and a custodian can cast them in his own time. Being made thin so as not to be confounded with the older work, they are easier to ascend and have a naïve elegance of their own unusual with concrete fittings. You may contrast this type of restored access with that installed by the Irish Board of Works towards the end of the last century to enable the visitor to St. Columba's house at Kells to reach the first floor, a structure exactly resembling a marine engine-room ladder.

Lay-out

When an ancient monument has been treated, it then needs to be laid out, in order that it shall not lapse again into the power of destroying agents, and in order that all its parts may be conveniently inspected (3, 10). The unregenerate ruin was noted for its deep nettle-beds and briar thickets. The Department has avoided a reversion to these not by weeding but by turfing all the wide open spaces, including the sides of the moats. For it is easier to keep the ground clean by the scythe and the motor mower than by the laborious process of hand-weeding. The system has a double advantage, for, while the wall-footings and vestigial foundations are kept clear for inspection a visitor can approach them comparatively dryshod on a wet day.

An important item in the scheme of lay-out is the marking of foundations discovered during excavation. This is done by outlining them in freestone set on edge in the new turf. By this means, when the plan of a building has been recovered, it can be perpetuated in full view, giving back to the ruins above ground something of their old status as parts of a single conception. The decayed monastery which before treatment is generally the most meaningless jumble, regains that orderliness that was, in fact, the keynote and background of the Rule. You now see the outline of the cloisters and how the church had transepts with apsidal chapels; the cream line running in the green sward gives you back the exact boundary between ground hallowed and profane. Also, by this means, you are sometimes able to see two periods at once, as at Tynemouth Priory, where the ghostly outline of the simple rounded apse of the Norman church seems gently to rebuke the grass-covered crossing of its ambitious Gothic successor.

It is chiefly in lay-out that the interesting cleavage between the ways of the Office of Works and the National Trust is most observable. The Department is characteristically Governmental in the uniformity that it imposes on its scheme of maintainence. Whereas every ruin ought

9 The Motte Mound at Pickering Castle, Yorkshire

10 The Castle of the Bishops of St. David's, as cleared and preserved by the Office of Works

11, 12 Preservation work at the Burial Chamber of
Bryn Celli Ddu, Anglesey

13   Excavating at Rievaulx Abbey

to have its special local character cherished if not exaggerated, the Department serves out to all the same type of bridge, of shed, of notice-board, of fencing. Nothing is left to chance from the first click of the turnstile to the last click of the lawn-mower so that you often have an embarrassing misgiving that romanticism has been not only preserved but sterilised, and its forlornness forcibly debunked by over-lawnliness.

The National Trust is saved from so much monotony and over-exuberance, partly by operating through local committees who still believe in the local traditions about their ruins and the old local pride in them. And this is as it should be, for history is as much a matter of places as individuals.

Although the Department has shown such excellent taste in the main, it has laid itself open to the charge of vandalism in a few instances. The site chosen for the custodian's house at Brougham Castle dwarfs the grandeur of that formidable gatehouse, and from an artistic point of view spoils a riverside setting of unusual beauty. Much the same thing has happened at Easby Abbey. But perhaps the worst of these discords is the combined museum and lodge at Richborough, which is placed in such a way as to neutralise the truly spectacular approach to the most imposing Roman relic which we possess; nor is this all, for the Department has installed a car-park in the nearer foreground.

Again, there is a tendency to arrange matters, giving preferential treatment to one historical period above another. Thus, the very charming little cottage that for nearly two centuries had been dovetailed into a corner of the ruins of Haughmond Abbey has been completely destroyed. I am not aware that archaeology gained anything by this demolition, and it is certain that the visitor of the present day misses a picturesque touch which added greatly to his pleasure, while the archaeologist of the future will think himself cheated of a period piece that he would have valued as much as the pure monastic work. Surely one of the best excuses for spending public money on the preservation of an ancient monument is that it should demonstrate the passage of history. In order to do that you cannot eliminate the freaks of evolution. They must be as sedulously preserved as the rest. The authorities will point out that this sentiment must occasionally be waived in the interests of archaeological research. Yet they removed a circular stone rostrum in the middle of the courtyard of Porchester Castle that was not in contact with any other building, and by whose demolition no discovery was looked for. The building was a bandstand put up in 1838 to commemorate the coronation of Queen Victoria. It had, in fact, been set up just twenty years after the last garrison had vacated the castle, which had been in continuous military occupation since the time when the Normans had built it in the corner of that old Roman fort. When the castle was thus finally deserted, the bandstand remained for nearly a century the only effective object of utility, being used for the most peaceful of all civilian demonstrations.

Here is a fierce heart which has beaten for a millennium and a half with military fervour, and, when it dies, its place is occupied by a rostrum for the distribution of sweet airs. The thing is a reincarnation of Samson's riddle, "Out of the Strong came forth Sweetness." Surely such an object had every claim on the regard of posterity, for metaphor in masonry is even more forceful than in print, since it is more subtle. A real sword beaten into a real pruning-hook would certainly claim a place in the most highbrow museum, but a battlement beaten into a bandstand is a greater trophy. But no! Your archaeologist of the early twentieth century will look with reverence on a Norman garderobe, but he cannot abide the sight of a Victorian bandstand. Yet, even now the radio is ousting local minstrelsy, and in less than half a century the Office of Works will be putting its stances on the Schedules.

CHAPTER II

The Primitives

THERE is a fascination about prehistory which is not unlike the lure of arctic exploration. Perhaps this is due to the impersonal nature of the mysteries which offer themselves for investigation, and also to a certain grand simplicity of lay-out in both backgrounds which, though they cannot be compared logically (any more than a chord of music can be compared with a colour), promote similar reactions in the mind and soul. No other monuments of archaeology have such a *constant* background as those of prehistory. They have but two habitats, the chalk and oolite downland with its crisp herbage and wide spaces of fragrant air, and the heather moorlands of fell, mountain, and cliff-top where the air is equally sweet, the sky equally large and the solitude equally prevalent. Why this should be so is, of course, easy to guess, as all the nations which successively occupied Britain prior to the Romans made their homes on the high ground only.

But the coincidence which places our most ancient and mystifying monuments quite naturally in the most lonely and beautiful places is so much like an act of historical justice on the part of Fate that it seems to add the sanction of a cult to prehistoric archaeology. And this feeling about it can be traced in the writings of all its exponents from the time when it was first suspected that any great artificial works could be older than the time of the Romans.

The impersonal aspect of prehistory presents a serious stumbling-block to the uninitiated sightseer who is sickened by endless displays at local museums of cases containing implements, weapons, and grave-goods of a monotonous similarity, arranged under labels which seem to stultify the imagination at first sight. It is hard to fix the mind on nations called for convenience "The Bronze Age People,"

13

"The Beaker Folk," or "The Stone Age Men," to whom one cannot attribute one single tribal name, or the name of one hero or villain, or indeed any word of human speech.

On the other hand, it is the very lack of these familiar tags, this spirit of anti-who's-who, which proves so irresistible to the other man, even if he is only slightly initiated, for it frees his mind from the gossip level of thinking in terms of the individual, and allows it to soar majestically among nations and cultures, while their time-spacing is unfettered by dates. You only allude to your time-spaces in round numbers—by centuries for the Iron Age, by thousands of years for the Bronze and New Stone Ages, thence backwards by names and expressions only. So that in prehistory the processes of history are reversed or, at least, transformed. Instead of a parallel of life with its events and facts you have something more like a parallel of religion with its symbols and types, the difference being that the objective of thought is not a hypothesis of what we may become, but the truth about a state from which we have become.

There is yet another aspect of prehistory which endears it to most of us. It is that there is still so much guess-work to be resolved that every student may think of himself as a pioneer. It may come his way at any moment to find something that will match a clue and solve a mystery. At worst he can hold a theory about this or that, or form a brand new one, and this is a pleasure as vital as artistic creation. A round of the ancient monuments, with very little reading, will give the merest layman ample material for one or more of such delectable flights. If, in the hopes of making a landing, he should set himself to study the question, he is apt to find himself not descending but driven to soar while the proposed destinations shrink away.

THE NEW STONE AGE

This goes equally by the label *Neolithic*. The doubling and trebling of terms, and the constant changing of them to suit prevailing fashion, is a sad weakness from which few of our modern sciences are free. Another drawback is the continual scene-shifting which has been going on since the

14   Remains of a Cotswold Long Barrow at
Notgrove, Gloucestershire

15   Timber strutting at Pentre Evan Cromlech, Nevern,
Pembrokeshire

16 Aerial view of Avebury, with Silbury Hill in the distance

17 The Ramparts of Bratton Camp, Wiltshire

War, and is still in full swing. In fact the Neolithic stage has been so much cleared since 1919 that only one large representative object has been left there—the long barrow. Even such vast tonnage as the circles of Avebury and Stonehenge which used to be regarded as bulwarks of the Stone Age have now been "carried forward" into the Age of Bronze, and the impetus which moved them has not yet subsided.

Neolithic man is now given about a thousand years in which to flourish. It pairs closely with the whole history of England from the Norman Conquest to the present day. Yet it seems only a short space when measured by a more remote standard—the time which the flint miners at Grime's Graves are supposed to have been at work. According to Mr. Reid Moir, who wrote the Office of Works Guide-book for Grime's Graves, operations were started there in 10,000 B.C., which is mentioned as a convenient outside date for the beginning of the interim period (called *Mesolithic*) that separates the old Old and the new New Stone Ages—a cool seven thousand being allowed for transition, the very time, in fact, which has lapsed between the building of the first long barrows in England and the setting up of the last war memorials.

A Neolithic Pot
[*Drawn by M. and C. H. B. Quennell*]

In spite of very intensive investigation and a meticulous examination of all clues not a great deal is known about the Stone Agers. They were agriculturalists, short in stature, flat of foot, and narrow in the cranium (*dolichocephalic*)—intellectuals, one suspects. They were the first people to introduce pottery here, and also to bring in the fashion for polishing stone implements. This innovation they practised in such an amazing way that the thing seems to go beyond mere pride in craftsmanship, and perhaps indicate those workings of the mind which promoted the ceremonial and ritual that is still the secret of the barrows

15

and their subsequent development into the stone circle. Of course the polishing of stone was primarily a mechanical (rather than an ornamental) amenity. It broke the flint-implement monopoly, because the invention of grinding enabled hard stones of igneous origin, such as diorite and jadite (which were not susceptible to chipping) to have a sharpened edge put on them.

There seems to have been something significant about the two principal implements of the period—the celt and the axe. Most of the best specimens surviving in museums have never been used, as if their purpose had been either ornamental or, more probably, ritualistic. Indeed the polished celt appears to be the symbol of the age, and perhaps it is not pure coincidence that the long barrow is shaped somewhat like it in plan and also in elevation. When you see it in the distance, on a high downland sky-line, its huge, smooth, whaleback shape suggests a great discarded weapon of the more primitive gods.

There are several interesting examples of the long barrow which are now being cared for either by the State or a local body. The most striking is Belas Knap near Cheltenham, which has been put into a state of preservation by the Department. This barrow has the characteristic long oval shape, with the blunt end facing (in this case) due north, a departure from the general rule of north-east orientation. Within the mound are two chambers, one of which is partly closed by an imperfect "porthole" entrance. Towards the southern point there are two passages which end abruptly without chambers. Exposed at the north end is a dry stone wall forming a concave crescent, in the midst of which is a portal opening on a shallow chamber.

This portal and the wall which makes a circuit of the barrow within the mound itself are two mysterious features which persist in the chambered cairn after its shape has been altered from an oval to a circle, and the Age of Stone has given place to that of Bronze. It is most strikingly seen in the great tumulus at New Grange in Ireland where it is adorned with a highly decorated threshold-stone carved with opposing spirals. The suggestion has been made that

18 Part of the stone circle, Stanton Drew, Somerset

19 Work on the great stones at Avebury

20   Trevethy Quoit on the edge of Bodmin Moor, Cornwall

21   Lanyon Quoit, Cornwall

even when it was not the true entrance of the tomb it was retained as the shrine of it where votive offerings might be deposited.

The neighbourhood of the Cotswold Hills on either flank of Belas Knap is our richest district in long barrows,[1] and they have been admirably dealt with in detail by Mr. O. G. S. Crawford in his *Long Barrows of the Cotswolds*.

Belas Knap, a long Barrow on the Cotswolds

The only other long barrow (still preserving its mound) which has been treated for preservation by the Department is at Capel Garmon in Denbighshire in North Wales. Like Belas Knap, it has a dry stone wall outlining its shape, built within the body of the mound, and at the wider end curving inwards to a false portal. This was orientated slightly north of east. The tumulus contains three chambers communicating with each other along the line of its axis, and these are entered by a passage from the south side.

At Cashtel-yn-Ard, near Maughold, in the Isle of Man, there is a very striking (though little visited) ruin of a long barrow, of which the only considerable part remaining above ground is the inward sweep of the stone enclosing wall on either side of the portal. Here, the horns of the crescent are not made of dry walling but of large stones set on end, while the forecourt which they embrace is paved. The portal, in this case, is closed by two large stones with a triangular

---

[1] Instances are Uley Barrow, near Dursley, and Notgrove in the Cheltenham district, illustrated (14).

opening between them. Five chambers in a line are placed immediately behind, to which there does not appear to have been any access from the sides of the barrow. A little way behind the fifth chamber is a small area on which a fire has been lit that burned with such intense heat as to fuse the stones. This barrow has the unusual orientation of west by north.

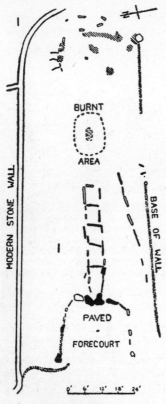

Plan of
the Cashtel-yn-Ard Long
Barrow, Isle of Man

Taking one step still farther to the west there are the remains of a long barrow at Goward, near Hilltown, County Down, in Northern Ireland, which seems to put a final emphasis on the sanctity of the portal and may give a clue to the nature of the change from the long and axe-shaped cairn to the round form. The ruin of the Goward barrow closely resembles that of Cashtel-yn-Ard, but it will be seen by the plan that the walls of the forecourt are not merely curved inwards so as to form a suitable approach to the portal, but are set out on the precise chord of a circle which seems to have been struck with particular relationship to the end of the barrow, which is not square to its axis but made purposely askew to it. This barrow, which was first examined in 1932, was pronounced by the excavators to belong to the Bronze Age, although the plan is definitely Neolithic. The evolution of those curves giving on the portal from two convex forms to one concave "conception" is at least striking, if not more significant.

The domestic life of the Stone Ager is not so attractive to

contemplate as that of his death cult and religion. The pit-dwellings of his settlements on Windmill Hill near Avebury, and at Maiden Castle near Dorchester have been exposed in recent years, although they are not of a nature to be preserved as an ancient monument. But the remains of the ditches

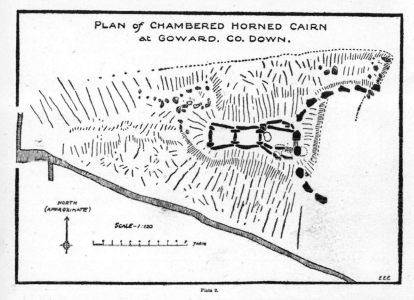

PLAN of CHAMBERED HORNED CAIRN
at GOWARD, CO. DOWN.

NORTH
(APPROXIMATE)

SCALE-1:120

Plate 2.

surrounding his settlements can be seen with their characteristic cross-causeways which make them conspicuously different from the fortification entrenchments of later peoples.

After the barrows, the most striking relics of the Stone Age are the flint mines in Sussex and Norfolk, and though these, especially the latter, have been well preserved they cannot logically be described as "ancient monuments." At Grime's Graves, near Brandon, one whole mine-shaft with its galleries has been put into a state of preservation by the Department. The place is rather a matrix than a monument, in which early man has left a precise impression of himself. Here you see him, not as a dreamy figure involved in speculations about the future life, but as a vigorous fact as hard as the floorstone flint which he conquered with his elementary tools and shaped into the instruments of our second civilisation.

THE BRONZE AGE

The new invader who had discovered in some foreign land first how to get copper out of the native rock and then

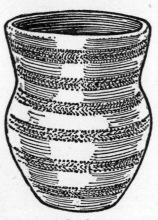

A Beaker

[*Drawn by M. and C. H. B. Quennell*

how to alloy it with tin (a much rarer metal) seems to have come suddenly into our midst at a date somewhere between 2000 and 1800 B.C. He is distinguished from the Stone Ager by two characteristics, namely by having a round instead of an elongated skull and by the possession of a vase-like pot of a particular shape called a "beaker." His arrival is signalised by a new funeral and religious cult of which the fundamental expression is a circle.

The beaker has proved to be one of the most useful identifications that any vanished race has yet provided, so much so that the name Beaker Folk is now given to the earlier settlers of this round-headed race. But the fashion for being buried with a beaker seems to have gone out fairly soon in favour of interment with another kind of vase called a "food vessel." This, in turn, gave place to a preference for cremation, when the incinerated remains of the deceased were put into a much larger crock called a "cinerary urn."

The three principal monuments of the Age of Bronze are the great and the small round barrows, the circles, and the alignments. The most intriguing (from a spectacular point of view) are undoubtedly the circles. In visiting these one gains the impression that there must have been either an astonishing number of cults of the circle, or a great diversity of opinion as to how they ought to be made. No doubt evolution played some part in this variety in size and design, but there is little to give one a clue to their respective ages, and one is confronted by the fact that local types are strong and do not appear to be mixed.

The plain circle of one ring made of moderately large stones is well seen at Keswick (27). A variety of this, having a large stone at the centre, is at Boscawen Oon in Cornwall.

The Rollright Stones, again appear to represent another type, for they are low in stature and very compactly placed. In Mid-Wales there are a number of circles which measure only a few feet across and are made of stones that do not stand more than a foot out of the ground.[1] Of quite another kind are the great circles at Mayborough in Cumberland and the Giant's Ring near Belfast. They are not made with standing stones but by a great solid rampart of earth or loose stones. In each there is an important central feature, at the Giant's Ring it is a cromlech, while at Mayborough it is a very solid monolith, which may or may not be part of one, though it does not look as if it is.

Compared with these the Wiltshire circles are so complex that they would seem to be the work of a different race of men altogether. Yet the two great ones of this group, Avebury and Stonehenge, do not appear to have much in common with each other except vast proportions. Avebury (19), the greatest of all prehistoric works in Britain, encloses within its huge circle twenty-eight acres of ground on which is built the greater part of a village (16). Within this enclosure are the remains of three minor circles aligned on a common axis, and the whole is surrounded by an immense ditch, and then a vallum made out of the excavation of this.

While speculation of all sorts has been busy with Stonehenge (24, 26) since it caught the eye of James the First on his way to Salisbury and he sent his court architect, Inigo Jones, to report on it officially, Avebury had remained comparatively unnoticed and wholly neglected until some time after the War. But in 1937 its restoration was taken in hand by Mr. Alexander Keiller and is still in progress. Already the great stone avenue which makes a mile long

---

[1] Examples are found on the slopes of Carmarthen Van and other hills between there and Plynlimmon.

approach to the circle has been treated; the fallen stones have been set up and holes where the missing stones stood (found through probing) are marked with small concrete posts. The finds from all these works and also from the Stone Age settlement at Windmill Hill (a mile away) can be seen at a museum in the village.

During the process of this restoration a very curious fact came to light. Although it appeared at first sight that most of the stones of the great circle had either been removed or broken up and were clean gone, it was soon discovered that no such thing had happened. Many of the stones were still there. They lay in graves which had been specially dug at some remote but uncertain date. Into these they had been toppled. In the course of re-excavating and lifting the huge pillars once more into place, the skeleton of a man was discovered. He was quickly recognised both as to date and also profession for, at the moment of his death, he carried on his person two excellent identifications; one was a coin of the time of Edward III, the other a probe such as that used by a barber-surgeon. It would appear from this that there was a keen circle-demolition party or a lord of the manor in Avebury in the fourteenth century which wanted to have the stones laid low (perhaps to spite the Devil), and that this little man undertook to do it. In a large number of attempts he was successful. But a nemesis (which had no doubt been foretold by the opposite party) overtook him. A stone, whose grave he was preparing, fell on him, and his followers made no attempt to salvage his remains. Thus, as he, himself, during his life, was the means of preserving so many stones intact, so, by the warning of his death, the legend of him was sufficient to keep a large proportion of the untouched stones inviolate. We may, in fact, owe not a little to the same legend, for the preservation of Stonehenge.

The main features of Stonehenge which are unique are (1) the trilithons which show well-made mechanical joints to enable the cross-pieces to remain immovable on the uprights—a matter of no small skill in masoncraft, to say nothing of the engineering feat of assembling such massive parts in position; (2) the horseshoe arrangement of the inner circles; (3) the appearance of the "blue-stones" which compose one ring and one horseshoe. They are made of a different rock from the rest of the monument, which is all of sarsen, found locally, and it was a long time before the place of their origin could be located. It has now been fixed definitely as the Prescelly Mountain in Pembrokeshire.

These blue-stones provide one of the most diverting riddles of prehistory. Why were they brought a good hundred and fifty miles to Stonehenge when the ground there was strewn with boulders of sarsen stone already conveniently sized by Nature? And how did they bring them? It may be some clue to an answer to the first question to remember that in a post-hole of the Sanctuary circle (p. 26) some pieces of Niedermendig lava from Germany were found and there are many other instances of like kind. But in each case the foreign bodies have been of a reasonably portable sort. The blue-stones can hardly have been brought such a distance except by sea, and the *Map of South Wales* published by the Ordnance Survey in their archaeology series goes so far as to indicate a possible route for the monoliths from their quarry to a loading berth in Milford Haven. So one has to face the fact that even if they were brought one at a time as cargo, the ship must have been a larger, more seaworthy, and more navigable craft than we usually give the Bronze Age shipwrights credit for. You can't go from Milford to the Salisbury Avon without doubling the Land's End and braving the open Atlantic for more than a hundred miles. Surely the blue-stones of Amesbury are among the chief monuments to human prejudice in the whole world!

Since 1925 three important discoveries have laid before us a host of new material relating to the riddle of the circles, though it rather tends to excite more and more conjecture than to get us any nearer a solution. In the middle of December of the above year Squadron Leader Insall, V.C., was flying over Salisbury Plain and was within sight of Stonehenge when he suddenly noticed what looked like the ghost of an exactly similar monument two miles away to the north of it. The Squadron Leader visited the spot on foot. He could detect some unevenness but none of those dotted rings seen from on high. He consulted Archaeology and was told that what he had been looking at was only a mutilated disc-barrow. The airman persisted, however, with the result that serious excavation was undertaken in August of the following year. The new Stonehenge proved to be a matrix rather than a monument and a very perfect one. One hundred and fifty-six post-holes were found arranged in six concentric circles (25). Or rather, the outer ones were circles but the inner ones developed an oval shape which assumed an axis exactly coincident with the dawn on midsummer's day—as at Stonehenge. The first riddle was: What sort of uprights had those post-holes held? Had they been Sarsen stones or blue-stones? Then it slowly dawned on the diggers as they examined the fillings that the uprights had not been made of stone at all but wood; there were traces of it even after a lapse of between three and four thousand years.

The site of this great find, which revolutionised at least one stock theory, was Durrington, and it is a great pity that the circle was not called after the place instead of being given the imitative hybrid name, "Woodhenge," which was not only a sin against imagination but against the science of place-names.

While the so-called Woodhenge was being explored an even more important dig was going forward in Anglesey at the ruins of the old cromlech of Bryn Celli Ddu (11, 12). This was being conducted by Mr. Wilfrid Hemp for the Office of Works. The discoveries here were positively thrilling, and it was found possible not only to make a thorough search (impossible where most of the chambered cairns have been concerned), but, when this was done, to carry out a virtual restoration both of the chamber, the passage, and the mound on top.

Bryn Celli Ddu[1] is a monument which nobody who is interested in prehistory ought to miss. Not the least interesting of the facts which came to light were those which substantiated so many theories of the older school of antiquity

[1] Englished approximately as Brin Kethley Dee.

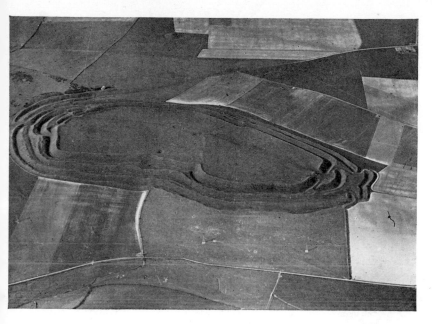

22 Aerial view of the fort from the south showing the
Iron Age (C) ramparts

23 The Western Entrance

MAIDEN CASTLE, DORCHESTER, DORSET

24. Stonehenge

who believed in the Druids—human sacrifice, the veneration of the ox and the serpent. There was also a stone marked on three sides with a design of meandering lines which makes everybody feel when they have studied them for an

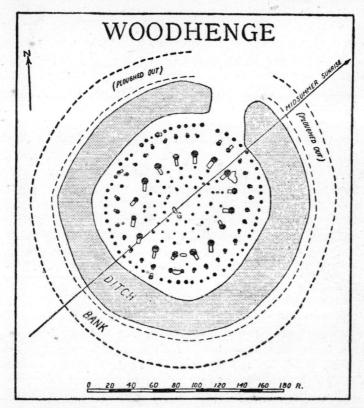

hour or two that they are within an ace of guessing something vital. This stone has unfortunately been removed to the National Museum of Wales at Cardiff. True, a replica is to be seen at Bryn Celli Ddu. But it is the replica which ought to be in the museum and the genuine object on the spot. You cannot mobilise sentiment on a replica.

By 1930 another "Woodhenge" had been sighted from the air in Norfolk, and people were beginning to found theories about the wood circles as distinct from the stone ones, when The Sanctuary was excavated. Its site had become almost a folk memory. It was right at the end of the West Kennet stone avenue which stretches for a mile from the great circle of Avebury, and in Stukeley's time two concentric stone circles had stood there. There was nothing to be seen of these in 1930, but after some difficulty the site was verified. Excavation revealed the sockets of the two stone circles, but that was not all, for several different rings of empty sockets were discovered which had evidently held wooden uprights. In fact, the Sanctuary was a *mixed* circle. The puzzle was heightened by the complete absence of a surrounding ditch as at Avebury, Stonehenge, Woodhenge, and even in that complicated structure at Bryn Celli Ddu.

So, in the last twenty years conundrums have increased out of all proportion to the solutions. Our gains have been in the field of comparative anatomy—plans of graves and temples, evolution links traced from the grave-goods of the dead and from potsherds out of the rubbish heaps of the living which point to a succession of cultural epochs. So much is this the case that there is a danger of prehistory becoming a purely technical mystery of whose joys only the expert can partake.

Happily there is another side to the whole subject which is neither baffling nor changeable like the archaeological aspect. It has an easy access for the ordinary sightseer and is likely to remain as long as ancient monuments of all sorts last. To illustrate what I mean, let us take the case of the *cromlech*. This object is the stony skeleton equally of the long barrow or great round barrow of the Bryn Celli Ddu type. The word, it must be admitted, has had hard treatment by the archaeologists, who have now entirely abandoned it. It has been in use for centuries in all parts of the British Isles to describe a characteristic table-like structure made by a huge capstone standing on a series of upright stones. The old theory (in vogue until the end of the nineteenth century) was that it was an altar on which the druids sacrificed to their gods. Unfortunately French archaeologists misunderstanding this word (which is of

25 Woodhenge, Wiltshire: concrete stumps marking the
positions of the original posts

26 Part of the inner horseshoe, Stonehenge: bluestones
in the foreground

27 Castlerigg Stone Circle near Keswick: Blencathra in the background

Welsh origin) applied it to the circle which, at the time, was also associated with druid rites. Then our antiquaries, instead of insisting on their native rights, gave up the term cromlech for the stone table and adopted a word current in Britany, namely *dolmen*. This was quite a good word in its way as it had a solemn and unusual sound. But when the conviction gained ground that the stone table had nothing whatever to do with druids or altars but was, in fact, the relic of a burial chamber, it became not merely an error to think in druidical terms but a positive intellectual crime. There ensued a violent pogrom of terminology, and the word *dolmen* was expunged with ignominy. To-day you must say *burial chamber* and nothing else.

It seems to me that from any point of view the change is for the worse. "Burial chamber" covers everything from a pyramid to a Victorian vault. But the name *cromlech* is specific, it only means one sort of thing. The theory of the moment as to what it used to be doesn't affect what it *is*. That is the point of view which the general observer ought never to lose sight of. The shape of the thing, its long continued poise for thousands of years and other attributes quite unconnected with any academic theory as to its origin are impressions that the imagination can react to more vitally when coupled with by an old name well devised and long tested in use. And you can enjoy the thing for what it is without the aid of one atom of archaeology. For this relic Anglesey is the happiest of all hunting grounds.

THE IRON AGE

It can hardly be doubted that our view of the Stone and Bronze Agers is tinged with melancholy from the fact that they left us nothing in monuments worth looking at except those of a funereal order. Even in their temples the focal points are associated with skeletons or incinerated young persons who often appear to have met their death in a violent manner under suspicious circumstances. Perhaps that is why we feel different towards the Iron Ager who, although he is the man who can boast of the real druid cult, did not leave us funeral monuments but those of a military and social kind. He is also much more humanised, as he bears a racial name (Celt) as well as a museum label, and in his last days we can even make contact with him through personal names and personal histories such as those of Caractacus and Cymbeline.

The principal monument of the Iron Age is the hill-top fort, marked on all the older Ordnance maps as CAMP, the most famous example of which is Maiden Castle in Dorchester (22, 23). Owing to extensive excavation, here and on other sites, our knowledge of the Iron Age has been enormously increased of recent years. It is believed now that this third great influx of peoples began to arrive in the seventh century B.C. Three waves are distinguished, labelled A, B, and C, and if you are at all well versed in Celtic fortress engineering you ought to be able to tell which wave built which fort by the arrangements of the entrance. These become increasingly complicated (22, 23) until the defences outside the gateway assume a maze-like form, and excavation has shown how mere gates have been supplemented by gatehouses, imitating the best manner of those Roman conquerors who were still afar off on the Continent.

These Iron Agers (A, B, and C) *alias* Celts, used to have a third and more popular name—the Ancient Britons. It was used by Froissart in the fourteenth century and, at the beginning of the present one, it was still the accepted label for our countrymen who opposed Julius Caesar. On his tomb in Long Burton Church, Thomas Winston, who died in 1609, describes himself as "descended of many ancient and noble houses both British and English." The name here used means Welsh, but the idea implied in the epitaph is that the Welsh are of the same stock as the pre-Roman-Conquest inhabitants of this country. That was correct, though it has since been shown that the Celts were a mixed nation of Welsh-speaking and Irish-speaking tribes. It was probably on account of this discovery of a split language that the respectable old name of Briton lost caste in the eyes of the scholar, who threw it to the journalists. These accommodating gentlemen found an immediate use

for it to describe an Englishman who was really a Scotch-
man, without causing offence to anybody's prejudices.

The curious result of these changes is that when the great
hill-top camps, which had long been a mystery to everyone,
were explored in recent years we heard a lot about the
museum aspect of the People of the Iron Age (A, B, and C),
but nothing human about our noble ancestors the Britons,
just because their name had become archaeologically and
scholastically taboo. They had, in fact, been put quite
unnecessarily to the same disadvantage as the Stone and
Bronze Agers. Nor did the excavators attempt to give us
any clue as to which artificial branch of the Celtic family
(P or Q) the various camps belonged. Perhaps they could
not, but it would have been a help to our family pride if they
had shown some interest in the matter. As they did not,
we have to be content with what guidance the river names
give us, namely that the Avons and Ogs watered the lands
of the Welsh-speaking[1] tribes and the Usks, Exes, and Axes
those of the Irish-speaking[2] clans.

Those Ancient Britons (or whatever you like to call
them) broke the monotony of our museum cabinets, if they
did nothing else. Since the remote Magdalenian Period of
the *Old* Stone Age (for which we have little enough to show
in this country) there had been no sign of art-for-art's-sake
on any of the multitudinous "finds." But art of a very
high order (so far as conventional design goes) is insepar-
able from all three stages of the Iron Age—though it should
be explained that this art is expressed chiefly in bronze
articles. Wherever a find from this period occurs, be it in
the humblest local collection, it is worth looking at. The
first enamels belong to this time, and it is believed that
the craft of enamelling is a British (in the true sense)
invention.

The Iron Age forts are among the most delightful of our
ancient monuments as they combine the work of Man and
Nature in equal parts, and do not require any "treatment"
to keep them from decay. In addition, they occupy situations on downland solitudes or cliff headlands which are,

[1] Brythonic.　　　　　　　　　[2] Goidelic.

as a rule, remote from human habitation; where the air is sweet and the grass short and crisp; and where gorse, bracken, wild thyme, and the blue sheep scabious grow with sublime fittingness.[1] One hopes that some of these sites will be left wholly unexplored and unrifled. For with that simple flora which seems devised to stimulate thoughts on destiny (to the accompaniment of the song of the lark and the drone of the bumble-bee) it seems a pity to break the essential spell of mystery for the sake of a chance addition to a branch of special knowledge.

[1] As examples may be mentioned among many Maiden Castle, Old Owestry, Cadbury Castle, Badbury Rings, the Trundle.

Celtic Brooch (Iron Age)
(Black Gate Museum, Newcastle)

28 The Roman Bath, Bath

CHAPTER III

Roman Occupation

AFTER babbling of *ages*, and then *millenniums*, and then *centuries*, prehistory suddenly snaps off short—within fifty-five years of a round thousand, and *history* begins with the first boatload of fresh invaders precisely at the date 55 B.C. In spite of that, there are no outstanding ancient monuments produced for another century, not, in fact, until the next Roman expedition despatched by Claudius Caesar in A.D. 43. It is significant of the power of the Romans and the assiduity of our archaeologists that actual traces of that landing, made in the very first year of the Claudian invasion, are visible, namely the defensive entrenchment thrown up by that pioneer landing-party. You can see it at Richborough, where it has been excavated and treated by the Office of Works. It is worth a long pilgrimage to gaze on such a trench—if you can chose a moment when there is neither a custodian nor a sightseeing crowd about the place. From the sentimental point of view, the finding and preserving of that ditch is one of the finest *tours de force* of modern archaeology. It is something to be able to stand there and look at it and reflect that, when it was made, only a few acres of Britain had been conquered by Rome, something essential to remember when you stand by Hadrian's Wall.

None of the contributors to our ancient monuments has succeeded in impressing the popular imagination so forcibly as the Romans. Not half a century ago the old gaffers of every village—who mostly couldn't read or write—knew how to ascribe every ruined wall or earthwork to the Romans. Even now, when we are sufficiently enlightened to know at a glance what is and what is not Roman, and though we are far enough removed from the heavy taste-bias of the Renaissance for classic things, that peculiar fascination remains. Relics of the Roman Period, whether they be of masonry, statuary, pottery or glass, have an unmistakable individuality about them which singles them out from the work of other people. They strike the eye with a degree of *pungency*—if one may borrow from the realm of taste and smell. The Roman flavour is one of magnificence compounded with a sort of ponderous banality. Yet, while it is so particularly individual as to be unmistakeable, it seems to have caught an essence of the Universal Mind, and in this way, even if we are utterly bored by it, it makes a special appeal.

With the exception of the splendid ruin at Bath (28), all the principal Roman monuments in this country are of a military or at least defensive character. The greatest is Hadrian's Wall from the Tyne to the Solway, which contains work of practically all periods from the year A.D. 122 till the end of the occupation (29, 31). Here, besides the remains of the Wall itself, there is grouped a number of forts in which the garrison was quartered. Owing to the desolate nature of the country these have been little interfered with except by the hand of time, and now that excavation has exposed their ruins down to the foundations (31), they give a unique picture of the life of the Roman soldier in Britain, while the immense number of finds that have been recovered can be examined in three museums along the line of the Wall—at Newcastle, Great Chesters (near Hexham), and Carlisle.

Besides the archaeological aspect of the Wall, it has a natural charm and often grandeur of setting in the Northumberland countryside that gives it a special character of romance. It reaches a climax in this respect at one point near Housesteads where it follows the crest of a cliff of black basaltic rock called the Whin Sill (29), which has a massive columnar structure, somewhat like that at the Giant's Causeway. From this crest the ruined wall looks out towards Scotland over a region of rolling fells with hardly a sign of human habitation. It is a most impressive place and becomes even more so when you examine that trench carved out of the adamantine basalt within the line of the Wall

30 The cross-shaped foundation at Richborough, thought to mark the position of the monument to the Roman conquest of Britain

31 Remains of bath houses at Chesters (Cilurnum) on the Roman Wall

33   The Amphitheatre, Caerleon

32   Remains of the Town Wall, Caerleon,

called the *Vallum*. This trench is not a military but a political relic; it was made to delimit the frontier not merely of the province of Britain, but of the Roman Empire itself.

Next in order (judged by their scale as monuments) come what are called the Saxon Shore forts. They were built at a late period of the occupation—some time during the fourth century—when the country was threatened by raiders of the un-Romanised parts of the world, notably the Saxons and the Irish (called Scots in our history books).

The idea of coast defence must have come as a novelty to the Romanised Britons, for, though their Celtic forefathers in Iron Age C had gone in for it intensively, the necessity had ceased at a time as remote from their day as the early Stuart Period is from our own. The prestige of Rome had been sufficient to guard all their boundaries without armaments except for that seventy mile stretch along the Border of barbarian Caledonia.

The Saxon Shore forts were built at intervals from the Wash to the inlet of Portsmouth. Of these, four remain in extremely good preservation at Burgh Castle (near Yarmouth), Richborough (Kent), Pevensey, and Porchester. All these are now under the guardianship of the Office of Works. Richborough (30) is the grandest ruin and the one that has been most explored. It was here (as noted above) that the Claudian landing was made, and it subsequently became the head port for the Continent. Within the walled enclosure is an immense concrete foundation shaped like a cross (30) which has given rise to the wildest speculations in all ages. The latest theory is that it was the base of a huge monument erected to commemorate the triumph of the Roman arms in Britain. It is dated as work of the first century, when it was firmly believed that Rome would rule the world for ever, and no such thing as a Saxon Fort was dreamed of.

Both at Pevensey and Porchester the fortifications were re-used by the Normans, who dovetailed their castles with the older plan but did very little to the Roman walls and bastions (8, 62–64). At Pevensey the rest of the enclosure

6

was used as an outer ward to the castle. But the fort at Porchester contains nine acres, and a Benedictine monastery was built there, so while the castle was self-contained within one corner of the Roman fort the rest became a monastic precinct, one of the Roman gates having been converted into a mediaeval gatehouse. The channel separating the Isle of Thanet from the rest of Kent was entered at Richborough, while the further end was guarded by the smaller fort of Reculver. This is also preserved by the Office of Works not so much on account of the Roman walling, the remains of which are scanty (34), but on account of the early Saxon church which was built within the enclosure in the seventh century (39).

Of the three legionary fortresses, York, Chester, and Caerleon, the first two, after a period of eclipse during the Saxon régime, regained their importance and became chief cities of Britain early in the mediaeval period. To-day they are both walled towns, though on an enlarged plan as devised by the Normans. Caerleon, the headquarters of the Second Legion, has sunk to the level of a small country town. It retains only fragments of the Roman walls (32) but possesses the finest specimen of a Roman amphitheatre in Britain (33). It was excavated in 1926, funds being provided by the *Daily Mail*, and put into a state of preservation by the Office of Works.

At Caerwent, only a few miles from Caerleon, is to be seen one of the finest stretches of Roman walling in Britain—the old south wall of the town, which has now received treatment and been made a national monument. Caerwent was the market town and tribal centre of the Silures under the Roman régime, and excavations there revealed one of the only two foundations of a Christian church associated with the Roman occupation. The other was at Silchester, the tribal headquarters of the Celtic Atrebates. The whole site of this once important town is now open agricultural land but the imposing ruins of its wall still enclose it.

Other fine specimens of Roman wall can be seen at Cardiff (a fort) where an attempted restoration (the only one) has been carried out, and at Colchester. Here, too, is

34

35 At York

36 At Aldborough, Yorkshire

ROMAN TESSELATED PAVEMENTS

37 Aerial view of the plan of the Roman Temple, Maiden Castle, and, inset, a view from the ramparts

38 The remains of the Roman lighthouse, with the Church of St. Mary-in-Castro, Dover Castle

the foundation of a temple on the Continental scale, and the only one of such a size known in Britain. It was used by the Normans in the eleventh century as the floor of their castle, from which at the present time access to the cellar-like, band-vaulted *podium* of the first century temple is gained. Otherwise, the Roman temples in Britain that have so far been discovered, are small and the remains of them are not impressive. Of the cult of Mithras (always worshipped in an underground chamber) an interesting example furnished with altars and votive emblems was found at Housesteads, on the Wall (now preserved by the National Trust). Much more complete, however, is the subterranean room in the garden of the Castle Park at Colchester. This is believed by many competent antiquaries to be a *mithraeum*, although the work is of an earlier date than "it ought to be" to coincide with accepted views as to when the cult of the Persian sun-god reached this country. At Chester there is an interesting rock-shrine (*aedicula*) to Minerva, with the figure of the goddess carved on the sandstone rock beside a neatly cut recess. It is thought that the carving may have owed its preservation to its having been mistaken for the Virgin Mary during the Middle Ages. If so, the image had better luck than that of the Fortuna of Marlborough (where a carving of this goddess was built into the west wall of St. Mary's Church). It remained in excellent preservation until the seventeenth century, when the Puritans mistook the wheel of Fortune for that of St. Catharine and forthwith defaced the interesting relic.

The Ordnance Survey map of Roman Britain shows the greater part of the country dotted thickly with sites of *villas*. These appear to have been houses of the yeoman farmer who was occasionally a textile industrialist with also a small dyeworks or a fulling and tentering plant—the Cotswolds (where villas are most numerous) was even then a sheep country. Nearly all the villa sites marked on the map have been excavated and filled up again. At Brading, in the Isle of Wight, the complete foundations of a villa, have been put under cover and, as this has particularly good mosaic pavements, the place is well worth a visit. But it

6*

is difficult for the imagination to replace walls and roofs and get an inkling of what looked like what in the old days. For this reason it would be helpful if one villa were restored.

The National Trust preserves a villa at Chedworth in a richly wooded hollow of the Gloucestershire Cotswolds. Here, one does not feel, as at Brading, any desire for a reconstruction. The ruin at Chedworth is supplemented by something in the spirit of its environment which makes its ruinousness more attractive than its reality can ever have been. There is something about the way in which those brown stones rise from their grassy terraces which stirs the imagination. The terraces slope to the south in a clearing of the thick and well-grown wood. Traffic routes are remote and other houses (bar the successor to the Roman farm) far off. The still air draws the warmth of the sun and the smell of leafmould from the forest. The *Pax Romana* has become a fixation.

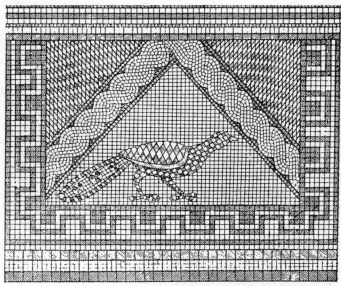

Portion of a Roman Tesselated Pavement at Wellow, Somerset

CHAPTER IV

Pre-Norman Period

IT is typical of the Roman Period that it is the only one which is precisely timed as to its beginning and ending. They came in 43 and they left in 410. After that we are landed in a sort of no-man's time in which the Celtic elements in Roman Britain come to the fore again and instead of combining to hold the forts of the Saxon Shore they follow the old game of local emulation. The P. Celts (Welsh-speaking) of the Forth-Clyde region descend on the Q. Celts (Irish-speaking) who are settled on the western seaboard, including the Isle of Anglesey. While the slaughter is going on between tribe and tribe, which had been good neighbours under the Roman rule, the Angles, Saxons, and Jutes are making almost unopposed landings in the Humber, the Wash, the Thames, and on the Isle of Thanet. This period (because it is temporarily obscure to the archaeologist) is given the name *Dark Ages*, which is a little unfair to people like King Arthur and his fellowship of the Round Table, and even more to the many shining lights who were saints in the Celtic Church.

EARTHWORKS AND CROSSES

The monuments of this time are principally earthworks and inscribed monoliths. Among the former perhaps the most typical are Wansdyke and Offa's Dyke. The former lies east and west and was actually built on top of a good Roman road. Some fine sections of it remain on the downs near Tan Hill, south-west of Marlborough. The ditch of Wansdyke is on the northern side of the rampart, so it was presumably built by a tribal group lying southward of it, but who they were and why they needed such a colossal earthwork, sixty miles long, is one of the mysteries of the Dark Ages. On the other hand, Offa's Dyke is a

37

comparatively well documented affair. It was built by Offa king of Mercia (eighth century) along the western boundary of his kingdom, which rested on the marches of Wales. It superseded (very advantageously for the Saxons) an earlier work of exactly similar type called Watt's Dyke, of which large fragments still remain. Although Offa's Dyke was only built as the western boundary of one of the seven Saxon kingdoms it remained the official boundary between England and Wales for centuries. One of the best views that can be had of it is at the little village of Mainstone in Montgomeryshire.

Christianity had come to Britain before the Romans went away, and was well established before the arrival of St. Augustine in 597. His mission was not to the British but the Saxons, and the two churches of Christ soon found themselves in competition. Accordingly, what the English historians calls the Early Dark Ages is known to the Welsh historians as the Age of the Saints.

The inscribed monoliths belong to this time, and in most cases commemorate notable people who held the Christian faith and observed it according to the traditional Celtic ritual and not as dispensed by the Pope. The stones are dated to the fifth and sixth centuries and, with a single exception, are confined to the western parts of Britain inhabited by the Celts (P and Q). Most of them are in the form of a rough monolith such as the prehistoric folk set up, and are often found in similar situations, mingling with a harmony that can only be described as poetical with relics of the Stone and Bronze Age nations in a setting of gorse and heather, accented by tints and tones of the never-changing sea.

The inscriptions are all either in Latin or Irish (Q. Celtic), sometimes in both languages. There is not a single example of a Welsh (P. Celtic) inscription known; those who used this language must have been still conversant with the literary forms of the old Empire and have preferred to use them for ceremonial occasions rather than the vulgar tongue. But one remembers that during the Roman occupation the careless scribblings of workmen on unbaked

39 Towers of the Saxon Church at Reculver, formerly preserved by the Admiralty as a navigational landmark, now under guardianship of the Office of Works

40, 42　Two views of Bewcastle cross, Cumberland, and (*centre*)
41　the Ruthwell cross

tiles (now dignified by the name of *graffiti*) such as "Austalis goes off daily on his own for a fortnight" are all in Latin. But the inscribed stones under discussion are all memorials. The monoliths stand five or six feet above ground and bear the Latin epitaph on the face of the stone and the Irish (usually) along one edge in characters of the Ogham alphabet, a unique script so elementary and logical that it looks like the work of one man's inventive genius, but its origin remains unknown. In addition, there is occasionally found a cross or the *chi-rho* symbol. The solitary example which does not come from the west was unearthed at Silchester. Leaving out of account Ireland (which is thought to be the home of the Ogham script), these stones abound chiefly in Cornwall and South Wales; North Wales has a number and the Isle of Man, and there is the group at Whithorn on the Mull of Galloway. Those with Ogham inscriptions are mostly confined to South Wales.

Many of the stones have been moved from their original sites and are either in churches or museums. At Margam there is a collection from the neighbourhood housed in a special museum built and maintained by the Office of Works. In these days, when such excellent casts can be made, it seems a pity to move the originals. If sentiment is worth nothing at the moment it is bound to come into fashion again, and we shall then count our losses.

The inscription on these stones in nearly every case is of the tersest sort, commemorating So-and-so the son of So-and-so without further comment. An exception is the Trescawen Stone at Llangwyllog in Anglesey. Although this was in Latin, it had never been properly read until 1935, when it was deciphered by Professor Ivor Williams the Celtic scholar, so in spite of its age (it is given an outside date of sixth century[1]) it must be regarded as a novelty which will upset many hastily conceived notions regarding the darkness of that age in Britain. The inscription runs thus—

". . . *iva*, a most holy lady, lies here, who was the very beloved wife of Bivatig (irnus), servant of God, a

---

[1] *Anglesey.* Royal Commission on Ancient Monuments.

bishop, and a disciple of Paulinus, by race a . . . .
udocian, and an example to all his fellow citizens and
relations both in character, rule of life, and (that) wisdom
which is better than gold and gems."

The seventh century saw the introduction of a monument
similar in intent to the old inscribed stones, but wholly
different in origin and craftsmanship from them. The cross-
shaft in the lonely, picturesque churchyard at Bewcastle on
the Cumberland Fells (40, 42) is cited as the first known
example and, for all we know, is the original of the whole
series.[1] The two striking differences between this type of
memorial and the earlier sort in the west are (1) that
they are the product of Christianity as re-introduced by
Augustine among the Angles and Saxons and not of the
Celtic Church, and (2) that they are the work of highly
trained craftsmen. Who these craftsmen were and in what
country they learned their art is quite unknown. The
mystery is heightened by the fact that these crosses are
confined with one exception to the Northern area, and (of
that date) are not known elsewhere. From this source, however, they spread to the whole of England, Wales, Scotland,
and Ireland. The exception mentioned is Reculver, where
a similar cross was seen by Leland in the sixteenth century,
standing within the old seventh century Saxon church between the nave and chancel. The fragments of this same
cross are now kept (but not well kept) in the neighbouring
church at Hillborough.

The type has come to be known as the Anglian cross.
Early examples, believed to be of near date to the Bewcastle shaft, are Acca's Cross at Hexham, the Ruthwell
Cross (41), for which a special apse has been built in the
parish church of that name (near Dumfries), and the Easby
Cross, now in the Victoria and Albert Museum, South
Kensington. The distinguishing features of all these are
the vine-scroll ornament, a classical rendering of interlace
patterns, and carved figures from the Gospels (43–45).

[1] There are two opinions on this and also on the question of date—seventh
century (A. W. Clapham), eighth century (W. G. Collingwood).

45 Fragment of a cross head in Durham Cathedral Library

43, 44 Cross fragments from Easby Abbey, Yorkshire

Although the Vikings were so destructive in the matter of church property when they first raided Saxon England, the Celtic Isle of Man, and Ireland, on conversion to Christianity they took particularly kindly to the cult of the high cross. They introduced new interlaced patterns in the design of it, and added to the usual Gospel series picturesque scenes from the old Norse sagas and fairy tales. The best example of this type of cross is to be seen in the Isle of Man, which was wholly under Viking sway until the thirteenth century.

In Ireland development came late, but nowhere else is the high cross seen in such magnificence. The principal examples are at Monasterboice and Kells. In Wales, development was also late. Here crosses were made elaborate, but were never of first-rate craftsmanship. In the North, the principal example is the Maen Achwyfan at Whitford (in Flintshire) which is preserved by the Office of Works. They are more plentiful in the south and an excellent representative collection of casts is in the National Museum of Wales at Cardiff.

In the west of Scotland there was a strong and very beautiful development, notably at Iona. But in the east of that kingdom, in the old land of the Picts, a third type of decorated memorial stone is found which is in a class by itself. The "symbol stone," as it is called, is a plain, undressed monolith like the old inscribed stones of Wales,

The
Maen Achwyfan
Pre-Roman Cross,
Whitford, Flintshire,
circa A.D. 1000

7

but, unlike them, it bears no clue as to its date. It is distinguished by having one or more of a range of symbols carved on it. They are highly conventionalised and very expertly carved, but it is impossible to tell what they represent—a hand-mirror? a shield and two spears? a crescent with broken arrow? a sea unicorn? There is also a plain animal series bearing respectively a bull, a wolf, and a dog. But although these are plain figures drawn with great spirit and artistic skill of the very first order, we are no nearer an answer. It is extraordinary that more attention has not been drawn to these early works of art. Anyone who is curious to see them will find their locations marked on the new Ordnance "Map of Britain in the Dark Ages (North Sheet)," which has recently been issued (January 1939).

To hark back to the Celtic Church, in which monasticism of a certain type (similar to that practised by the Coptic Church in Egypt) was such a strong feature, nothing monumental has remained to us except what has recently been discovered on the headland of Tintagel. Here an ancient religious settlement which may go back to the sixth or even the fifth century was unearthed in 1935. A strong tradition relating to King Arthur has long been associated with this headland. However, when it became apparent to antiquaries that the ruins of the castle were not earlier than the Norman period the suggestion that Arthur had anything to do with any part of Tintagel was pooh-poohed by the learned. But the king may, after all, have a triumphant come-back when the excavations at present being conducted by the Office of Works on the Headland are completed.

Of monasteries of the Roman orders belonging to the Dark Ages, the best relic is that built by the Venerable Bede at Jarrow. It remains with its nearly perfect Saxon church in a secluded and peaceful precinct beside the Tyne, in spite of the ravages of its neighbourhood by industrialism and industrial depression.

Of the late Saxon period the principal monuments are all churches, and so are not within our purview.

42

48, 49 Two sides of the same stone in Heysham Churchyard, Lancashire

50 In Gosforth Churchyard, Cumberland

HOGBACK GRAVESTONES

51 A native Welsh castle, in Ewloe Woods, Flintshire.
The keep and eastern moat

VIKING AND NORMAN

Although the Norman period sets in with a conquest date
as suddenly and precisely as that of the Roman Occupation,
namely in 1066, it should not be forgotten that the Normans
were really Vikings who had changed their name, habits,
and language, and were actually blood brothers to the Danes

"The Saint's Grave," a Hogback in Gosforth Churchyard

who had previously conquered England and were settled
in the old partition called the Danelaw. In fact, England
was beset by Scandinavian influences, for the Norsemen
held the leading Irish ports, the Scottish islands, and the
Isle of Man. Yet none of these peoples left any but the
scantiest legacies in monuments, whereas their cousins, the
Normans, who had sojourned for a couple of generations in
France, gave us in a century and a half a more solid collection of permanent works than the builders of any other
period.

Perhaps it was that the Scandinavian people were essentially workers in wood, carpenters and carvers. One
gathers this from the one purely Scandinavian ancient
monument that we have. This is the hogbacked gravestone
of which there are excellent examples at Heysham (48, 49),
in Lancashire, Gosforth in Cumberland (50), and Hickling

in Nottinghamshire. Like the Anglian crosses, they have not yet received the attention from the public which they deserve. These stones lack the pretentiousness and conventionality of the great crosses, and there is something touchingly child-like about their conception and freedom of treatment that makes one think of the woodworker who

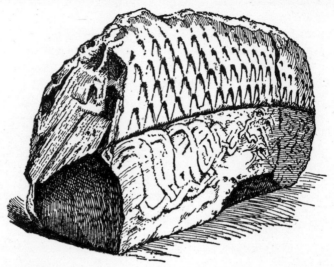

The "Warrior's Tomb," a Hogback in Gosforth Churchyard

had only momentarily given up his friendly medium to make something in another which would last for ever. The hogback appears to be the imitation of a house roofed with wooden shingles; the sides are covered with pictorial designs, while the ends are often seen to be embraced by two muzzled bears.

The Normans, themselves, although they pursued such a strong policy of building in stone, retained many traits of the woodworker. They had a passion for smooth surfaces, well-dressed stone, good ashlar, and a type of ornament that was always decorative rather than architectural.

There was a curious *fait manqué* about the Scandinavians. They had the opportunity of forming an empire which would have bid fair to replace the fallen one of Rome, but they never seem to have given such an idea a moment's thought. They conquered parts of Gaul, Italy, Sicily, England, and secured the whole of Iceland. It is more than likely, too, that they planted a strong colony in Greenland. Yet each conquering band kept its own territory, and as there were no ties of confederacy with a mother land, the claims of kinship were not kept up. But the Normans had learnt one thing from the Roman Empire in their attacks on its towns, namely that stone buildings withstand fire, and that was an invaluable lesson for any conqueror to learn, especially if he intended to make and hold his conquest by the church as well as with the castle.

CHAPTER V

Castles

LIKE all Norman architectural works the castle was, no doubt, imitated from Roman fortresses seen on the Continent, and two of the first castles to be raised in England are especially Roman in conception and design. These were the White Tower in London and Colchester Castle. It seems odd, and contrary to the usual laws of evolution and progress, that nothing so big should ever have been built again after the eleventh century. ▾

But the real novelty, and the instrument whereby the conquerors ensured their hold on the country, was not the big castle but the little one—mere "vest-pocket" size. This was made in the good old Scandinavian way out of wood, a dangerously inflammable material. But the structure could be rendered comparatively fireproof if it were mounted on an earthen pedestal which could not be set alight. Thus you had a wooden tower perched on a mound or *motte* (by which name this elementary kind of castle is still known). The mound not only afforded protection against fire but was very difficult to assault, as anyone will find who tries to walk hurriedly up either of those typical mounds at the castles of Carisbrooke or Pickering (9).

The motte castle was usually accompanied by a double enclosure in the form of a figure of eight in which retainers could find bivouac quarters and men and beasts could seek safety if there was sudden hostile demonstration on the village protected by the castle. These enclosures formed an outer and inner bailey,[1] their earthen banks being defended by stout palisades of wood. The mound with its

[1] *Bailey, ward, court,* and *courtyard* are interchangeable terms. In general usage *bailey* is popular for Norman castles, *ward* for thirteenth century and mixed period castles, *court* and *courtyard* for fourteenth-century castles and later.

54   Conway Castle, Carnarvonshire, showing unique arrangement of main entrance

55 Framlingham Castle, Suffolk

56 Rhuddlan Castle, Flintshire, by the River Clwyd

tower was placed astride the palisaded bank of the inner bailey. From the top of the tower, archers could command the whole system of fortification and, if the enemy succeeded in entering the inner bailey, favoured members of the garrison could still enter the tower and hold it as a last resort.

EVOLUTION OF THE CASTLE

In the twelfth century there was a general move to consolidate the castle by replacing the wooden structure on top of the mound with a stone building—the familiar Norman *keep*. The name seems to refer to the state apartments, the place where the lord of the castle or the constable *kept* (meaning *lived*). The word still goes on at the older universities, "Where does So-and-So keep?" and in ordinary parlance you "get your keep" as part of a bargain, meaning your lodging.

The word is used in a more specialised sense referring rather to fortification than lodging where a *shell keep* is alluded to. This was a more compact form of citadel plus inner bailey. It came into use in a few places in the twelfth century. The mound was made larger and wider and a circular wall built so as to accommodate wooden buildings round the inner side with a small courtyard in the midst. An example of the smaller type of shell keep is seen at Farnham Castle in Surrey, part of the fortified palace of the Bishops of Winchester, now preserved by the Office of Works. The larger kind is well seen at Berkeley and Restormel in Cornwall (Office of Works monument).

Another variety was the round keep (sometimes called a *Juliet*): examples of it are Strongbow's Tower at Pembroke Castle and the Norman Tower at Windsor.

Although the square keep was never again made of such a size as in London and Colchester, it was sometimes a very imposing affair, at Middleham (72), for instance, and Porchester (62). This type is built with a massive cross-wall to carry the flooring, and access is closely guarded by having the entrance on the first floor, to which an outside stair is led through a barbican that exposes any unwelcome

47

guest to a concentration of bowshot and missiles. Such an arrangement is known as a *forebuilding*, and is seen in its most complete form at the Tower of Newcastle.

The next important change in castle-building came in the thirteenth century, when the wooden palisades and earthen banks surrounding the baileys were replaced with stone walls, in which round towers were placed at intervals to sweep the intervening spaces of the *curtain* (as the new system of walls was called). In the older castles the keep was retained, but in the newer ones, built by Edward I in Wales, in the latter part of the century, this feature was abandoned and, instead of the smaller towers which had been built purely for the defence of the curtain, large towers took their place for the double purpose of sweeping the walls, and providing lodging for officials, their households, and retainers.

At the beginning of the fourteenth century two minor changes are noticeable. One is the introduction of *machicoulis*. This was a permanent translation into stone of a wooden contrivance that had originally been thought of as a temporary measure in time of siege for securing a more efficient defence of the curtain. A wooden gallery was built out on *brattices* (which may be equated with *brackets*) so as to overhang the wall. Through holes in the floor bowshot or missiles could be directed vertically on the enemy who might be trying his hand with a battering ram, a mine, or a scaling-ladder. The wooden gallery was replaced by making the wall-walk oversail the parapet on stone corbels. It was a favourite defence for the tops of towers and looked so handsome that it was adopted for the sake of appearances and finally formed a conspicuous feature of the romantic Gothic builder of the eighteenth and nineteenth centuries.

The other development was in the gatehouse. Instead of being a mere portal, it was made the principal grand feature of the castle. While the difficulties of ingress were increased by extending the portico till it became a sort of inner barbican and was given a second portcullis, the upper works were at the same time made more roomy and

57 The exterior from the west

58 Interior of the Hall

CAERPHILLY CASTLE, GLAMORGANSHIRE, SOUTH WALES

59 Dunstanburgh Castle on its Northumbrian headland

60 Holy Island Castle, Northumberland, across the strait

magnificent, till the King, lord, or constable of the castle was attracted from his old quarters in the inner ward to take up his abode here. At Beaumaris, Harlech (67), Kidwelly, Brougham, and elsewhere, the gatehouse with the principal state apartments of the castle is a fortress in itself within the line of the walls, an inevitable hark-back (morally, if not mechanically) to the original keep.

By the middle of the fourteenth century the various ideas which had been expressed in different castles seem to have been edited, with the result that a more logical standard plan was produced, of which Bodiam Castle in Sussex (National Trust) is an excellent example (71). It seems an odd fact (though not inconsistent with experience) that in spite of the efficiency of military architecture at the end of the Edwardian period, compared with what it had been a century before (when it was first emancipated from the motte-and-bailey tradition) it had never got rid of one deep-rooted idea, namely, that certain ranges of essential buildings within the wards were beneath the serious attention of a fortress engineer, that they were *temporary* works— mere carpentry. The new plan was to incorporate all these detached buildings of the castle into a single architectural scheme. It was to be done by carrying continuous blocks of buildings round a courtyard and thus forming a building like the quadrangle of a college at one of the universities.

The fifteenth century is a barren one so far as new castles are concerned, but in the sixteenth Henry VIII found it necessary to revert to a national precaution which had not been taken for over a thousand years—systematic coast defence. His castles, which stretched from Kent to Cornwall, were the first in this country made to resist gunpowder artillery. They were partly reminiscent of the castles of the mediaeval period and partly they foreshadowed the forts of a later date. Two fine specimens at St. Mawes (68) and Pendennis have been put into a state of preservation by the Office of Works.

8

CASTLES AS NATIONAL MONUMENTS

The castle has always been an exceedingly popular monument. In the Victorian age it had a reputation for waking extravagant sentiments of romance. This was fostered by the then "ivy-mantled tower," by stories of languishings in dank dungeons, of hidden treasure, and of subterranean passages. Votaries expressed their feelings and discharged their vows by eating sandwiches among the ruins. But now, the scientist, taking the place of the romanticist, has had quite a long innings. Under his tutelage the castle has been remorselessly scoured both of ivy and legend and the public is invited to turn its attention solely towards the scientific angle of every stock and stone. But this outlook, together with the newly treated walls and excavations, has become somewhat mellowed while, willy-nilly, romance is stealing back to its old haunts in the rejuvenated ruins. Of course, as a sightseer, you get the best value out of a castle if you can hold both points of view at once, and yet not be too much preoccupied with either to be blind to the direct reaction of the monument (which an artist would think the *only* important one), that is, to the actual shape of the thing and how this shape fits into its setting and environment.

I will draw up a rough list of our castles with an eye to their individuality rather than their technical points.

CASTLES OF THE SOUTH

Dover Castle has, perhaps, the most striking combination of natural and historical setting. It has a Norman keep which can boast of a thickness of wall which is probably unequalled—twenty-five foot in the lower courses. In this tower, the Lord Wardens of the Cinque Ports kept their state and their watch upon the Channel. From here, in quite ordinary weather, you can see the coast of France clearly—a blue loom over the sun-fret of the eddies in the narrow tideway. It gives you a handle to history about which there is no pageant flimsiness. Hubert de Burgh and his famous sally from Dover on the fleet of Eustace the Monk becomes modern history when you look at the

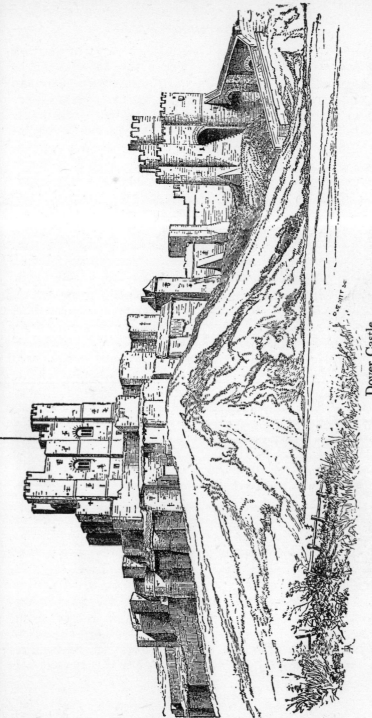

Dover Castle

Roman lighthouse that must have been a thousand years old in those days (38). It stands adjacent to a Roman building long since converted into a Christian church. All stand together within the huge enclosure on that green hill-top above the white cliffs, which is surrounded by thirteenth century masonry presenting itself with the most theatrical note of that period when you cross the moat. But the place is no mere museum piece. It is alive still and has its garrison; and the bugler, when he sounds the last post against a wild sunset over the chops of the Channel, blows the Roman and Georgian periods into one.

Like Dover, Pevensey (8) and Porchester (62–64) are both built within Roman forts, but in these two cases the walls were so perfect that the mediaeval engineers included them in their schemes of defence without thinking it necessary to make any great alterations. At Pevensey two sections of the Roman wall have fallen, but the rest is intact, and in very much better repair than the twelfth century keep of the Norman castle. Only the base courses of this are left to indicate that it was made on a unique plan comprising many apses. The whole of the Norman enclosure was buried in débris which, in places, exceeded the height of a man. When the Office of Works was clearing this away in 1935 they came upon what one might describe as a really popular find. This was an assorted pair of mediaeval dungeons in perfect condition. How thrilled the older school of antiquaries would have been!

We are told by the purist that the word dungeon should be properly used only for the keep of a caste (which he prefers to spell *donjon*) and what the tourist and romancer loves to call a dungeon ought to be called a prison. This, however, is quite unscientific, for the Oxford English Dictionary cites examples supporting the tourist's point of view from as far back as the twelfth century ("So wel is me in this doel doungeoun"). The Pevensey dungeons I have described as "assorted" because they are each typical of a particular kind which perhaps represents the first and second division of baronial imprisonment. In the one case you are privileged to walk down a set of steps to your noisome destination, where you are granted the amenity of being shackled to the wall. In the other case you are deposited in a bottle-like crypt which has no egress except through a hole in the ceiling, and instead of being honourably fastened to the wall you are secured ignominiously to a bolt in the floor. Here the water of the moat (which is also the cesspool of the castle) will come and keep you company when the winter rains cause it to rise. Archaeologists used to be fond of protesting that the popular idea of the dungeon had been greatly overdone. Modern excavation has proved the reverse to be the case, even where such a kindly disposed man as a bishop was lord of the castle.

Porchester (62–64) has a glory of its own. This is partly, but not wholly, concerned with scale. If the mediaeval castle, which occupies an area of sixty-five yards by forty-three, had stood on its own ground it would have looked a very large and imposing building. As it is, it appears tucked away in a corner of the Roman fort. This is a perfect square, two hundred yards each way enclosing, that is, nine acres. In the corner remote from the castle stands the church of the Augustinian priory, otherwise the grassy expanse is uninterrupted. Some of the chief expeditions against the kings of France have been mustered here. Even to-day, immediately you pass through the eastern gate of the fort you are on the seashore (62); an encroaching tide laps the footings of the Roman fort at high water and the old embarkation quays, together with the outer defences on the eastern side, have long since been washed away. But on the north side the salt water creeps up into both the Roman and mediaeval ditches. There is nothing here but green banks, saltings, and fields lying under the rim of the South Downs. The bustle of naval affairs has moved down the inlet from Portus Adurni to Portsmouth (carrying the first part of the Roman name with it for prestige). It is this end-of-the-world quietness, contrasting with the scale of the monument, which gives it the other part of its glory.

In the South Downs a curious geological phenomenon occurs in which rivers take short cuts to the sea through the midst of the hills instead of having to find their way round them. It is due to the erosion of a watershed that was at one time higher than the Downs. The effect of this feature is to pierce a natural coastal barrier with a series of gaps like mountain passes, likely to afford tempting opportunities for hostile landing-parties. Accordingly those lords who owned broad acres in the Weald behind the Downs built castles in the gaps. Thus, the very ruinous Bramber and the still magnificent Arundel. The case of Bodiam is somewhat different. It is built so far up the course of the Rother among the hills that the object must have been to escape attention rather than to attract it. That fourteenth century castle of the courtyard type (preserved by the National Trust) is one of the most charming ruins we have (71). Its appearance from the outside is nearly perfect and is beautified by reflections in the lake which surrounds it—a picture graced by water-lilies. There is no feeling of over-preservation or too much lawn-tidiness about the place. Even the well-stocked museum is as homely as it is interesting, and does not distract from the romantic environment.

Carisbrooke Castle still preserves something of its ancient state, being the residence of the Governor of the Isle of Wight. The more ancient parts have been treated by the Office of Works, and are open to the public. There are three unusual features in this castle. As at Pevensey and Porchester, the Norman castle has been raised in the corner of what was believed to be a Roman fort. The Roman ascription, however, has now been called in question, for it is thought that the fragments of masonry exposed are not Roman but Celtic work—an advanced bit of pre-Roman culture carried out late in Iron Age C. The second feature is the ring of fortifications of the bastion type with which the mediaeval castle was surrounded in the reign of Queen Elizabeth. It is an early example of the new and revolutionised type of bastion fortress that was coming into vogue on the Continent, where it developed rapidly until it culminated in the works of Vauban. But there is only one other considerable specimen in this country—the town walls of Berwick-upon-Tweed. Both were built by the same

Italian engineer, Federigo Gianibelli, who was actually engaged in fortifying the Thames when the Spanish Armada was expected.

The third thing is more generally known, namely the wheel whereby water for the castle is lifted from a deep well. It works on the principle of the wheel in a squirrel's cage and was originally intended as a fatigue for prisoners. Since the supply of prisoners ceased it had been worked by a donkey and two of these animals are now kept for the purpose by the Office of Works.[1]

Except those two castles of Henry VIII's coast defence scheme, at St. Mawes (68) and Pendennis in Falmouth Harbour, and the shell-keep castle at Restormel, already mentioned, there are no important castles in the west country preserved as national monuments. Nunney is more like an extra large peel-tower, and the bare relic at Tintagel can hardly be called important except in the annals of the romance of King Arthur which is henceforth (as explained on p. 42) more likely to transfer itself to the Celtic monastery on the headland than to the castle, no part of which can be older than the twelfth century. Of the unpreserved ruins in that quarter, Okehampton is the most complete and interesting, having all the glamour of the bats-and-ivy tradition.

In this brief survey it is impossible to do any justice to the CASTLES OF THE MIDLANDS AND EAST ANGLIA. But Framlingham must have a mention, as it is unique. It was the head-quarters of the Dukes of Norfolk—Bigods, Mowbrays, and Howards—until the beginning of the seventeenth century. Approaching the place you see a vast fairy-tale castle made like a shell-keep on a gigantic scale, with walls forty-four feet high set with thirteen embattled towers (55). You enter this enclosure through a majestic gateway, expecting to see the ruins of the largest castle in England. Instead, there is nothing on the wide expanse of grass (now kept in velvet trim by the Office of Works) but a very post-mediaeval-looking building. A house; yes, but not the home of the premier Dukes of England—a workhouse. Of course as an ancient monument, a workhouse built in 1729

---

[1] A more detailed account of these wheels is given in *Curiosities of Town and Countryside*, by the same author.

has its points, and if you are a romantic and like to see a noble ruin in really bad repair for the sake of the contrasts it presents, you have something even more telling here at Framlingham Castle. The originator of the idea lies in his tomb in the parish church among those splendid sarcophagi of the Howard Dukes of Norfolk—Sir Robert Hitcham, a law officer. He bought the castle in 1635 and left it to Pembroke College, Cambridge, with instructions that the buildings of pomp within the walls should be demolished and the proceeds devoted to the poor. Perhaps it was his intention to have almshouses built with the materials to keep his name in remembrance. At any rate the Civil War ensued almost immediately on his death, and nothing seems to have been done for a century. Afterwards they relieved the poor by building them a workhouse within the enclosure of the 44-foot walls. However, even the shell which is left is one of our grandest monuments and well worth a visit.

And one cannot leave out Orford Castle (52), an eighteen-sided Norman keep whose turrets look out over the deep-water roadstead of Orfordness, where great fleets loitered and foregathered in old days. And Thetford should be remembered for possessing what is perhaps the largest and most impressive motte mound in the country, though nothing remains on top of it.

The famous lake castle of Kenilworth has recently been placed under the guardianship of the Office of Works and is now being treated. Its associations with Simon de Montfort and Walter Scott's novel have not saved it from becoming a sad wreck. Its greater neighbour of Warwick is still owned and resorted to by the Earls whose forebears earned so many high places in history. It is the only castle with an original working portcullis which is still lowered at dusk every night. The castle is one of the most unaltered in general appearance that we have and the public are admitted to parts of it.

CASTLES OF THE NORTH

Immediately after the Norman Conquest (when the sister of the Saxon heir to the English throne married the

61 Bamborough Castle, Northumberland, above the North Sea

63   The Monastery Gatehouse

64   The Water Gate by the sea

62   The massive Norman keep

King of Scotland) Yorkshire became the cockpit of Britain. In 1136 the Scottish Border rested as far south as the north bank of the Tees. Yorkshire was therefore within easy

Conisborough Castle, Yorkshire (roof and chimney restored)

striking distance. Even when the Border was put back again to the Tweed, raiding parties from Scotland frequently penetrated as far south as Doncaster. Doncaster Castle has gone, but a few miles away is the very striking Conisborough.

9

It is little visited owing to its being in the middle of a black country of collieries (between Doncaster and Sheffield) but it has a very fine Norman keep of unique design and stands magnificently. This keep is circular, tapering outwards at the base. From this batter six half-round buttresses rise which have the appearance of turrets. In spite of neglect the building is in a good state of preservation, and it seems a thousand pities that such a rarity in military architecture should be allowed to decay when many less important buildings are being preserved as ancient monuments.

In York itself, only one important feature of the castle is left. That is Clifford's tower, another curiosity. York is one of the few castles which were installed with two motte mounds. Clifford's Tower stands on one of them. The mound was raised by William the Conqueror, himself, in 1068, but the tower belongs to the early part of the fourteenth century. Its shape is that of a quatrefoil, and the only other building which it is known to resemble exactly is a tower at Étampes in France. Mr. St. John O'Neil has described it as "a small residential tower" and has compared it with the keep at Dudley and that compact little castle in Somerset at Nunney (53). By a clever piece of detective work he has demonstrated that the Early English arcading in the chapel has been salved from an earlier building and re-used; there must have been an earlier building still—the scene of the massacre of the Jews in Richard I's reign.

The great tower of Knaresborough (also of fourteenth century date) is rapidly tumbling to pieces. A little further North is Richmond Castle, one of the most striking in point of situation. It preserves an original gatehouse and hall of the Norman period. The Office of Works took this building over just in time to save the eastern curtain wall, which was slipping bodily over the precipice. The measures they adopted to secure it are among their major triumphs in the art of treatment.

Richmondshire (to use the older name of the district, which still persists), one of the richest agricultural districts in Yorkshire, is situated where Swaledale opens from its

Conisborough Castle, Interior of the Chapel

narrow defile among the Pennines into the Plain of York. A few miles over the ridge from Richmond is Wensleydale, in the entrance of which two fine castles are situated. Middleham Castle (Office of Works) has one of the largest Norman keeps in ground plan, though it was not carried up for more than two storeys (72). It is surrounded by a range of buildings in the manner of the courtyard castle to which access from the keep was gained by means of a bridge—an unusual plan. Personal interest centres round the castle in that it was held by Richard, Earl of Warwick, the King Maker, in the height of his power. It was from here that Edward IV made his escape while being kept prisoner by the Last of the Barons.

A few miles higher up the Dale is Castle Bolton, a four-teenth century courtyard castle, more sumptuous in its appointments than Bodiam. It was the home of the Scropes, and for some time the prison of Mary Queen of Scots, whose room is still shown. The castle is not a national monument, but is in excellent preservation and accessible to the public. In appearance and in setting it must rank as one of our most romantic castles.

Spofforth was the first North country home of the Percies when they migrated into the stricken area which the Conqueror had laid waste after the rising of Earl Waltheof. Nothing is left of the early residence, but a hall of later date built by the Percies is preserved there by the Office of Works—Spofforth Castle.

Three other Norman families grew to power in this neighbourhood and produced men who controlled the destinies of mediaeval England and Scotland; the Bruces of Guisborough, the Nevilles of Brancepeth and Raby, and the Balliols of Barnard Castle. This brings us into County Durham, the old Prince-bishopric, in which the King's writ did not run. On this account it was said to harbour many villains who were fugitives from the justice of the English courts. However that may be, it is certain that it acted as an efficient buffer state against the raids of the Scots, as the true peel-towers do not begin until you enter Northumberland, where they abound. Durham Castle, the ancient seat of the bishops, was given up by them a century ago and converted into a university. But the old buildings have been very little altered and the public are admitted. A very cogent reason why the Scots behaved more tenderly towards the people of Durham was that the Bishop had an advance post in a detached part of his county palatine. This was at Norham on the banks of the Tweed itself—the scene of Scott's *Rokeby*. The castle has a very grand aspect, its massive keep towering over a bend in the Tweed. The Office of Works have got it now, and are making the best of a sadly battered remnant. That it possesses a wonderful series of mason's marks, some of which are unique, is an odd irony.

The Scottish Border was divided into three zones for purposes of defence, known respectively as the East March, Middle March, and West March; and "Warkworth and Naworth and Merrie Carlisle," were, respectively, the principal strong points. Warkworth was the headquarters of the Percy family after they came north from Yorkshire though sometimes the sister castle of Alnwick was the residence of the head of the family—the Earl of Northumberland. Naworth was the home of the Dacres family, a well-preserved building, still a private residence.

Conditions in the East and Middle March depended on the loyalty of the Percies and Dacres and other owners of private castles, though there was a royal garrison at Berwick. But Carlisle had always been a royal castle, though its constable had to face a peculiar difficulty that was unknown in the east, owing to the fact that between the Solway and the Cheviots there was no proper boundary between the two kingdoms. A stretch of no-man's land lay there which neither side had ever been able to partition, as both claimed an overlap. Consequently this Debateable Land was lived in by outlaws from both countries who sold their services as raiders and assassins to the highest bidder. As a rule, all three marches were placed under one official head called the Lord Warden of the Marches.

Of all the Border castles Bamborough, which cuts the figure of a Continental chateau, is perhaps the grandest. It stands on a rock platform of black basalt between the village it once protected and a sweep of the sea (61). But Warkworth is the most interesting and is one of the first buildings that the Office of Works took over after the War. Its Norman keep was replaced in the time of Edward III with a great tower that was in keeping with the taste of the time (which was considerably in advance of the twelfth and thirteenth centuries, both in ideas of art and luxury). On the outside of this tower is carved a huge lion rampant (the Percy lion of Brabant) which strikes the eye as soon as you enter the village and look up the street to the castle standing on top of the hill. From the middle of the tower a high, slender turret like a minarette gives you a wide sweep of the surrounding country, commands the little seaport of Amble, and scans the sea-line beyond Coquet Island. The old thirteenth-century gatehouse that was standing at the time of Harry Hotspur is in excellent condition. Associated with the castle is a hermitage and chapel hewn out of the sandstone rock. Its carved work is of much interest—even the window-tracery of the period being imitated.

On both sides of the Border the peel-tower is of common occurrence, all manor houses at one time having been built on this plan, and even parsonages (as witness Corbridge old rectory and the Deanery at Carlisle) though a licence "to crenellate" had to be obtained from the Crown in each case. The type is derived from the early Norman castle, though the earthen motte is missing and the bailey becomes a simple stone enclosure called a *barmekyn*, made as a pen for cattle in times of a raid. West of the Pennines the range of the peel-tower extends right down into North Lancashire. On the Scottish side of the Border it ranges up into the Highlands, the difference being that in England it was only needed as a defence against the Scotch, whereas in Scotland it was the clan of the neighbouring valley that was more to be feared than the English raider. The majority of towers on both sides of the Border are of fourteenth and fifteenth century date, though they retain all the essentials of the original Norman keep.

But there is one remarkable castle in Northumberland

which does not appear to have been built with any idea of defence against the Scots. This is Dunstanburgh (59). Like Hadrian's Wall (29) and Bamborough (61), and the small castle on Holy Island (60), it is built on a mass of whinstone or black basalt of semi-columnar formation which makes so spectacular a platform for a ruin, and Dunstanburgh, even in its fragmentary state, is one of our most picturesque ruins. The rock and its castle stand out into the sea between sweeps of sand that are unusually sparkling and silvery in texture, and the sailor-folk have long known it by a characteristic name of their own which is still recorded in the official *North Sea Pilot*—"The Snags of Dunstanburgh." It was built by that rash and romantic person, Thomas of Lancaster, who is said to have been imbued with the spirit of the Arthurian legend. He openly defied Edward II, and succeeded in arousing the weak king to the one passionate act of daring recorded of him, with the result that Thomas lost his head within sight of his own castle of Pontefract.

Had Thomas gauged the King's spirit better or matured his plans more wisely, Dunstanburgh would have been ready to receive him at the dangerous moment. As it was, the castle, when completed, came in for only one exciting adventure, when it was held by a Lancastrian constable for Margaret of Anjou during the Wars of the Roses. But the King-Maker, who took up his quarters at Warkworth and engaged Alnwick, Bamborough, and Dunstanburgh all at once, reduced all three with cannon and then held a feast at Dunstanburgh. No more stirring tales are told of it. All the same, it is a castle of romance.

There is nothing so grand on the west of the Pennines as the Northumberland castles. Carlisle is still a regimental depot, which gives it a living link with its old military days. The Ancient Monuments Department of the Office of Works have taken over the great daunting keep built by William Rufus, and adjacent ancient parts of the castle. The Normans sited their fortress on the rising ground just behind Hadrian's Wall. It came in more handily for them than a quarry. They pulled it all to pieces, and those parts

63

of the town wall which stand show Norman buttresses built of stones shaped by the Roman legionaries.

The broken shell of Penrith Castle has been put into a state of preservation; so has its neighbour at Brougham, a fine ruin where there is much to see. Like Brough Castle, a little farther south, in Westmorland, it is built in the angle of a Roman fort, though not to such advantage as those castles in the south, the Roman ruin having merely given the Norman builders a flat site and foundations for a portion of the walls; though no doubt the strategic points were of equal value to both builders. At any rate, the view from the top of the keep at Brough is particularly fine, ranging from the Pennine summits to the principal Lakeland hills.

Brougham has one of the most formidable entrances of any of our castles, though the approach to it is highly picturesque, an effect which has unfortunately been much modified by the placing of the new custodian's house. On the very top of the keep is one of the most beautiful little chapels in any castle. Brougham was a favourite residence of that great dame Lady Anne Clifford, who kept the state of a queen during the greater part of the seventeenth (our most democratic) century. Among her virtues was a passion for restoring castles—and she owned a large number. If it had not been for her assiduity there would have been much less left of Brougham than there is. Her tomb with the display of heraldry, showing at large her illustrious connections, is in Appleby Church.

The Welsh Castles

The history of the Conquest of Wales is twofold, and has given us two very different types of castle. The first phase developed immediately after the Battle of Hastings, by which victory William only secured Saxon England, which was bounded on the west by Offa's Dyke. The Normans did not anticipate much difficulty in completing the conquest of the island, and the process was handed over to three newly created earls who were given large grants at the three principal strategic points of the Border, Hereford, Shrewsbury,

65 A Doorway, Durham Castle

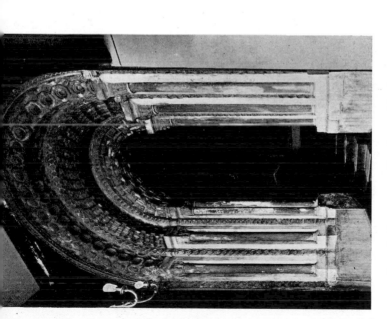

66 The Lower Chapel, Dover Castle

ENRICHED NORMAN DESIGN IN CASTLES

67 The elaborately defended entrance, Harlech Castle, North Wales

68 St. Mawes Castle, Cornwall, a coast defence work of Henry VII

and Chester. The first, William Fitz Osbern, contented himself with building a castle at Chepstow just across the Dyke, on the far bank of the River Wye. Here he consolidated his building and his sphere of influence. Earl Roger de Montgomery of Shrewsbury made a much more adventurous bid, marching through South Wales to Cardigan, on the coast, and establishing two motte castles on the way—one at Montgomery (called after his native town as Smith of Liverpool might call a trading-post he has established *Liverpool*) and one at Llandovery. All these mottes remain, including the one at the starting point in Shrewsbury. Roger halted at Cardigan, but his son, Arnulph, made friends with the local Viking element, which had established itself at the mouth of the Teify, and took a long-ship down to Milford Haven, where he founded Pembroke Castle, which became the nucleus of a Norman-Flemish colony that still calls itself Little England Beyond Wales.

In the North, Earl Hugh Lupus of Chester trekked along the coast and built motte castles at Rhuddlan (56), Carnarvon (69), and Llciniog in Anglesey. This last remains, and is a fine example of its kind. Independently, Fitzhamon and his twelve co-adventurers set out from Bristol and took over the old Roman fort at Cardiff in which, according to the fashionable plan, they built a motte and made use of the Roman walls by earthing them up and erecting a palisade on top. Then, according to the old story, Fitzhamon's knights set out to colonise Glamorganshire, and their names are associated with the present castles there.

All these expeditions seem to have met with unprecedented success, which was probably due in part to the prestige of the Norman victory at Hastings over the Saxon, that ancient enemy who the Welsh had come to regard as unbeatable. The novelty of the Norman knights, with their equipment, efficient military formations, and, above all, their "vest-pocket" castles, must have been overpowering. In addition, there was the language of this new conqueror which (being of Latin stock) resembled the Welsh in so many ways. Then there was a courtesy and tact about the newcomer which was wholly lacking in the Saxon and accorded well with Welsh ideas as to how a civilized nation should behave. Above all, the Normans helped them in their internecine wars, which appear to have been unending since the departure of the Romans. In 1081 the great William himself had gone the whole breadth of the country to pay his vows to the patron saint at St. David's. From the Norman point of view this surplus of country beyond Offa's Dyke was a godsend, for the English lands would barely go round to pay for services at Hastings. Here was an opportunity to say to any disgruntled knight. "Well, you'd better try your luck in Wales. You can keep what you can get there and I will confer on you the powers of a count palatine. No questions will be asked from London, providing you acknowledge me as overlord."

In 1098 the Welsh recovered from their surprise at these goings-on and, for the moment, gave up their own quarrels and united in a national effort to send the new owners of England back over Offa's Dyke. In this rising their success was swift and almost complete. Only one castle held out in the heart of the country, namely Pembroke, which was commanded by Arnulph's steward, Gerald de Windsor, father of the great race of Fitzgerald, whose name was to resound in Ireland. That this one castle did hold out saved the prestige of the Norman adventurers and enabled them to make a gradual return. Within half a century they were not only back, but well established in South and mid-Wales. But they did not get a footing again in the mountainous parts of the North, now represented by the counties of Carnarvon and Merioneth, until the end of the thirteenth century, when the Edwardian castles were built, which are in a class by themselves.

There was but one royal castle in South Wales, at Carmarthen, of which only the gatehouse remains. The rest had all grown out of private enterprise in the motte-and-bailey days. It is not surprising, therefore, that the great charm of the Welsh castles is the infinite variety of them and the individuality which constantly makes itself manifest, added to the grandeur of the situations in which some of them are set. Yet, as compared with the North, only a few have been made national monuments, of which the finest is Kidwelly.

On the other hand two of the largest castles, Caerphilly (57, 58) and Pembroke, are actually being rebuilt by private owners. One cannot help being a little sorry that Pembroke should have been subjected to this bold experiment, as it was a very interesting as well as a fine ruin, and the new work now being carried out on it (which at best must be guess-work) is certain to close the door on any further archaeological research in this particular quarter. The same criticism may be aimed at Caerphilly, though the case is rather different, and the result may justify the loss to archaelogical research, because, when finished, it is bound to give an unusually striking idea of what a great castle looked like in the old days, an impression which only a very well-read mind and unusually vivid imagination can supply on materials offered by a ruinous site.

Carew Castle in Pembrokeshire is still in the unregenerate state though, in appearance, it is one of the grandest castles in Wales. It stands full height, a formidable block like the old French Bastile. Yet, while its outlines are all in the grimmest manner of the thirteenth century, the wall spaces are relieved by airy mullioned windows inserted by an Elizabethan owner (Sir John Perrot). The effect must have been garish indeed when the windows were new, but now they help to fill the picture with a sad, melting beauty that an artist would find it hard to resist.

Still, in spite of the romantic trails of ivy that we should have lost in the process, I could have wished that the Office of Works had taken over Carew rather than Cerrig Cennin Castle (70), that ought not to have been tidied up one jot, for it was certainly the wildest castle in the grandest setting in Wales. From across the narrow valley its battered towers mounted into the skyline from natural bastions of the limestone rock. Few people ever found it, for its fame was not trumpeted in tourist programmes, and its almost guaranteed solitude was part of its charm. When you gained admittance to the empty ward which in its latter days had been a stronghold of a robber band, you found a doorway in one corner which led to an embattled stairway leading down the cliff (far above the tree-tops in the narrow valley), down to a natural cave in the face of the precipice in the depth of which the castle well had been dug. And there was a certain awful dankness about those steps which the authorities are bound to "treat" and get rid of as, through treatment, they got rid of the bloodstains on the block in the Tower of London. No! No! Science is good, but the castle fan must have his morbid moments—it is part of the fancy.

Another castle which owes much of its grandeur to its situation on top of a limestone cliff is Chepstow, which cuts such a splendid figure in the lower gorge of the Wye. As already mentioned (p. 65) it was founded by Fitz Osbern, Earl of Hereford, and though the son of the founder got into trouble and lost his estates, the castle was given to that very steady and thoroughgoing family of de Clare which also became owners of Pembroke Castle, from whence the most famous of them, Richard "Strongbow," sailed to conquer Ireland. In some ways Chepstow is the finest of all the castles of the Marcher barons. For though it is not so massive or in such good preservation as Kidwelly it has a great deal more in the way of architectural refinement, a quality, the very lack of which gives Kidwelly the sturdy ruggedness which is its essential characteristic. But the owner of Chepstow in all its periods took a pride in firstrate masoncraft and carving, which was no doubt much more readily available here than further west; even so, it is of a more imaginative kind than you find in an English castle except in Northumberland. The castle with its four wards is strung out along the cliff, having the great keep in the centre and an imposing gatehouse at either end, so that no other fortress shows off all its parts at once to so great an advantage. A large part of the town wall is also intact, and the place keeps its pride and its charm as well as any in Wales. It is still in private ownership though open to the public.

Chepstow is in the ancient province of Gwent, which tallied closely to the present Monmouthshire, a county named separately from England and Wales in state papers, and one in which Border feeling has for centuries been more characteristic than anything definitely Welsh or English. The "Three Castles" are in Upper Gwent and are a type of their own (at least two of them are,—White Castle and Skenfrith). White Castle stands on top of a hill and is miles away from anything like a village, which is really significant of the purpose it was built for, namely, short periodic occupation when danger was afoot. In spite of its grandeur of appearance, the inner ward being entered between two of the most browbeating drum-towers imaginable, there is no sign of comfort anywhere—no house-pride. It is a mere man's barrack-blockhouse, and its masculinity is as grand as it is primitive. The Office of Works has put it into a state of preservation.

Skenfrith is just such another, in point of plainness, though on quite a different plan, and is surrounded by a very quaint and picturesque village, for it has amenities of situation wholly lacking at White Castle. The National Trust preserves the castle, and I hope it will never see fit to abolish the pretty orchard which grows within the walled enclosure about the circular keep, and provides a genial shelter for the cows in the summertime.

The third of the three castles is Grosmont. Unlike the other strategic centres it was made liveable by Edmund of Lancaster till the time of the great Duke, John of Gaunt, whose name is still remembered in local stories. But before Edmund's time it seems to have been a residential castle and the town a prosperous borough deriving its support from the castle. The most striking feature to the casual glance is a tall fourteenth century chimney with a top architecturally treated in the best manner of the Decorated Period. The castle has been put into a state of preservation by the Office of Works.

A little to the south of this district (on the road from Monmouth to Abergavenny) is Raglan Castle, called in Welsh saga "The Yellow Tower of Gwent," the home of the family of Herbert. The ancient tower is a hexagonal keep and the rest of the castle is late fifteenth century, built in the reign of the first Tudor King. It is more like a palace than a castle, yet it stood a bitter siege in the Civil War under the command of its owner, the grand old royalist Marquis of Worcester. Even in its ruin this castle has an innate charm that is like a personal touch. In the chaste beauty of its masonry it has no equal among castles, and its situation in the breezy Monmouthshire uplands is so much in harmony with the ruin and its mood that one feels here is a monument that has been made to match its environment and could not have been so built anywhere else.

At the head of the Vale of Usk, where the old road from the coast goes up to Brecon and the country of the upper Wye, is Tretower. It is a perfect visual example of the evolution of the manor house, for you have the castle with its round keep and walled enclosure, in which the family lived from Norman times to the end of the thirteenth century. Then, a couple of hundred yards away, you have the house to which they migrated when times were safer and more modern ideas had made them regard their peel-tower as a pokey hole. On the new site you can follow the fortunes of the family in their still more expanding ideas down to the eighteenth century, when, in spite of its succession of added amenities, the dwelling was looked on as old-fashioned and was sold out of the family—that family which the acres of the manor had nurtured since the days when a knightly follower of Bernard de Newmarch had come there at the end of the eleventh century and erected his motte.

CASTLES OF NORTH WALES

The penetration and virtual conquest of Mid- and South Wales had been carried out with a series of smash-and-grab raids by the Normans, for which the English were not responsible. The Conquest of 1282 was a very different matter and was really the result of the Barons' War, in which the Welsh had taken sides with the rebel Simon de Montford against the English crown. Although Simon's principles, to begin with, were excellent, he was prepared,

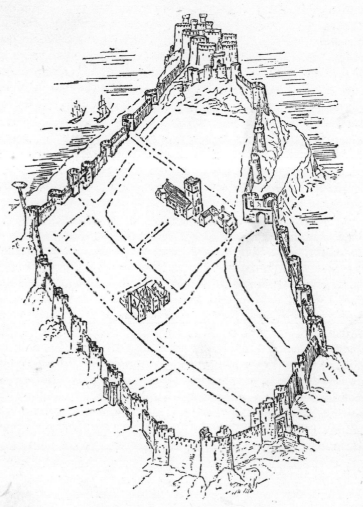

Conway Castle and the Town Walls

This sketch, from Clark's *Mediaeval Military Architecture*, is not strictly
accurate, but gives a good idea of the lay-out and area covered

in the end, to sell his country to keep himself in power. At Pipton, in 1265 it was Llewelyn, Prince of Wales who was the buyer. It was small wonder, therefore, that when Edward I began to govern, he should take the first opportunity to inflict a humiliating treaty on Llewelyn. This was made at Conway in 1277. The treaty was broken, war ensued, and the Prince of Wales was killed. Edward saw clearly that the only way to ensure peace was to unite the two countries, whether they liked it or not. This he proceeded to do by building a number of impregnable castles in key positions in North Wales and attaching to the more vital ones "free boroughs" in the shape of fortified towns stocked with English populations to supply the needs of the garrisons within the castles.

Edward began building castles in that part of Wales between Conway and the Dee that had been ceded to England by the Treaty of Conway. The first was at Flint, the second at Rhuddlan (56). This was in 1277, five years before the Conquest. The work was undertaken by the best engineers and skilled craftsmen that could be found, based on the experience of two centuries of castle-building in Britain, and gleaned by personal observation in the Palestine crusade.

At Flint a keep is seen for the last time. It is an "improved" keep, not placed in the line of the walls or even within the enclosure, as in the older castles, but outside the wall of the inner ward—approached by a drawbridge over a sea-water ditch. Here it could act not only as a last resort, if the rest of the castle fell, but provide a means of escape at discretion. At Rhuddlan the keep was wholly given up. The plan is concentric. The inner ward has walls of immense thickness and height. It is square in shape with two entrances, one at each opposite corner.

The war ended in '82 with the death of Llewelyn and the following year Conway Castle was begun. This exactly fits the top of a great rock and is a masterpiece of efficient planning, differing in many ways from all the Edwardian castles, and its ruin is, from the aesthetic standpoint, the most picturesque (54). The building of Carnarvon (69),

69 Carnarvon Castle from the sea

70 Cerrig Cennin Castle, Carmarthenshire, on its crag

Beaumaris (7), and Harlech (67) followed quickly. At Conway, Carnarvon and Beaumaris, walled towns were included in the plan, and at the two former the walls survive; at Conway the town walls are quite complete and offer the best example of a mediaeval walled town in Britain, if not in Europe.

Carnarvon is the largest of the castles (69) and the one in which the most sumptuous residential quarters are provided, while over the great gate is a figure of the king seated in a niche (probably Edward II, for it was finished in his time). Indeed all the appointments of this castle are on the grand scale, and it would seem as if it had been intended to make it a capital palace of the Principality where the new English Prince of Wales could hold his court. That this title should be a mere appanage of the crown was probably far from the intentions of Edward I. But the outbreak of the new war in Scotland distracted him.

The appearance of Beaumaris (7) suffers from its lowlying situation. But the recent clearing and reflooding of the moat (since the Office of Works took it over) has made a great difference to its good looks. It differs from the other castles in having so many rooms built within the thickness of the wall, and it is a perfect example of the true concentric castle. A charming feature is the small dock where ships could enter from the sea and unload within the shelter of the defences.

Harlech is austere and has the most tremendous gatehouse of them all (67). Its situation in the sweep of Cardigan Bay is an immense asset to the scenery. A gaunt fortress on a sea-girt crag with its back to the mountains, its towers catch the eye thirty miles away when a wheeling sunbeam lights them up.

Harlech has stood more than one memorable siege, but the most interesting incident in its history is its association with Owen Glendower, who succeeded in wresting the castle from the English and occupying it. Owen made Harlech his headquarters, and under the title of Prince of Wales wrote letters from here to the Pope and the King of France. One thing which stamps Glendower as being a man of great ideas is the thoroughness with which, in spite of his harrassed life, he attended to details of the regalia of his assumed princedom. In Paris is preserved an impression of his great seal taken from a letter addressed from Harlech Castle to Charles VI, King of France. The design and craftsmanship are as good as any seal of that date in Europe. In 1923, when the courtyard was being cleared by the Office of Works, a bronze harness boss was found bearing in enamel the arms of Wales as assumed by Owen Glendower. But when the castle was taken back by the English, after one of the most bitter sieges, Glendower's family was there and that of Sir Edmund Mortimer, who stood so near the throne of England, and who had married Glendower's daughter. This lady and her children died in the Tower of London from the effects of this siege.

There is one other large castle in North Wales which has been put into a state of preservation by the Office of Works, at Denbigh. Here there is also an interesting old town wall which has within its circuit one of the most portentous specimens of a thirteenth century drum-tower. It guards a well and is a perfect subject for one of those moonlight arabesques of the Bats-and-ivy Period. Called the Goblin Tower, it still looks the part. The castle and all about it resembles the lord-marcher type of South Wales castle rather than the government fortresses built by Edward along the coast. It was, in fact, built by "private enterprise" like the Castles of Chirk and Ruthin, Edward having given sufficient inducement to Henry de Lacy, Roger Mortimer and Reginald de Grey, respectively, to have these works carried out.

The Welsh, themselves, were backward in masonry of all sorts and built very few castles larger than the motte-and-bailey type which they soon imitated from the Normans. The best relic is in the wood of Ewloe near Northop in Flintshire (51). This is under the guardianship of the Office of Works, as is also that picturesque peel-tower in the Lledr Valley, Dolwyddelan Castle, the birthplace of Llewelyn the Great. But the most romantic of the castles built by the Welsh themselves, and also the most mysterious,

71 Bodiam Castle, Sussex

26. Mud Loam Castle, Yezd, Iran

is Castell-y-Bere near Abergynolwyn. It was built on the grand scale in the mid-thirteenth century by Llewelyn the Great. The situation is on a rock in a flat valley between two steep spurs of Cadr Idris in one of the grandest situations in Wales. Only the overgrown stumps of the ruin are left on the rock. Very little is known about this great vanished glory. It is not near any important place, nor does it guard any important pass or ford. Why was it built? Surely there can be but one answer. It was meant to overcome that time-honoured bugbear, the antagonism of the Waleses, North and South, to each other. Here, on the very border was to be the nucleus of a new capital for all Wales. The castle was made, but the town on that excellent (but still desolate) site about its base was never built up and consolidated. Towns and even villages were abhorrent to the Welsh. Perhaps the settlers never did back up their prince and then, in less than half a century, it was too late; North and South Wales still distrust each other profoundly, and there is no true capital to the Principality yet.

Of the CASTLES on the WELSH-ENGLISH BORDER nothing has been said. The best example that has been put into a state of preservation is Goodrich in Herefordshire (Office of Works) (2, 3). Stokesay, near Craven Arms, is a charming ruin, in a good state and well looked after, but this should rather be classed as a fortified manor house (made to look as castellated as possible) (100). Ludlow is the largest relic. It was here that the Council of Wales was held.

There are any number of green earthen mottes and small castles in Shropshire and Herefordshire. Many of them, quite interesting relics, do not even receive a passing mention in the guide-books and are only found by exploration, which gives them a heightened value.

This account would not be complete without mentioning the "bishops' castles." Most of them were palaces for which licences "to crenellate" had been obtained, and they had been made to look like castles, though it was not seriously expected that they would have to stand a siege. A few were actually fortresses, among which was the castle of the prince-bishop of Durham already referred to. Farnham

Castle has also been mentioned (p. 47). Another is at Llawhaden in Pembrokeshire, now under the care of the Office of Works. This belonged to the Bishop of St. Davids, and was occupied by him as the lord of a great manor rather than as a prelate. He had palaces in the semi-fortified style at Swansea, Lamphey, and St. Davids. There are fair remains of all of these, but that at St. Davids is much the most perfect and has been put into a state of preservation by the Office of Works (10). So has the interesting ruin of Bishop Robert Burnell's crenellated palace at Acton Burnell in Shropshire. This Bishop of Bath and Wells was chancellor to Edward I, and built the castle-palace at Wells which is still surrounded with its enceinte walls and moat.

CHAPTER VI

Monuments of Religion

IN our days, when time is thought to be so much more precious than it used to be—though nobody can tell you why—sightseers are apt to rush from one kind of ancient monument to another without making any effort to change their personal frame of mind. This is a great mistake, especially if that change be from the military to the religious monument. The essential difference between these two great classes is that monuments of the military type are real museum pieces, out-moded, dead relics of the art of defence about which we have become so much more enlightened than we used to be. But monuments of religion and the background of religion, which is death, have never been out-moded. Though they may be broken or overgrown with weeds they represent something which is alive, something whose source and destiny we haven't really become any more enlightened about than we used to be. Even such radical changes of fashion in our methods of approach to the Deity, such as the Reformation and the rise of Nonconformity will be ratified by history as experiments rather than improvements.

Another point in comparing the two great classes is that the military monument is never beautiful except by accident (unless it is partly domesticated like Raglan Castle). But the religious monument sets out to be a thing of beauty in every part so long as a traditional standard of good taste was observed by the builders. And it remains a thing of beauty in spite of all changes of fashion.

CROSSES

The cross is the most compact and, at the same time, representative monument to the Christian religion that we have. In spite of its great simplicity as a symbol it has been made to reflect all shades of religious thought from the time that the Romanised Celts were fighting the Saxons in this country down to the great war-memorial building days of 1919. The study of the crosses as a whole has been very much neglected both by archaeologists and tourists, though it seems to be becoming more popular, and both the Office of Works and the National Trust are protecting a number of them as national monuments while a great many more are on the Schedule.

The principal varieties are as follows:

1. The Memorial Cross
2. The Churchyard Cross
3. The Preaching Cross
4. The Market (or butter-) Cross
5. The Boundary Cross
6. The Signpost Cross
7. The Calvary

The earliest crosses were commemorative memorials and would seem to have been an elaboration of the rough-hewn monolith, the idea of which still appeals to the imagination. Possibly the cross-head itself was not an adaptation of the Cross of the Crucifixion but the conventionalised chi-rho symbol which as early as the fifth century had begun to augment the Latin legend on the inscribed stones.

As mentioned in an earlier chapter (p. 40) the art of the decorated cross-shaft seems to have blossomed out suddenly in Northumbria in or about the seventh century. There seems to be no link of evolution between these and the earlier inscribed stones that were merely marked with the chi-rho or with a cross in a circle. So it is thought that the first of these —perhaps the Bewcastle Cross itself (40 42), was made by a foreigner imported by Archbishop Theodore. Or was it done by a native trained abroad? The mystery has not been unravelled. The outstanding fact is that nothing like these Northumbrian crosses has been discovered abroad. So the native tradition counted for something!

The Northumbrian type of cross continued in vogue until

75 Head of the churchyard cross, Tyberton, Herefordshire

73, 74 The Eleanor Cross, Northampton

56 The Market Cross, Chichester

the Norman Conquest when it was definitely looked askance on as a sign of the barbarous culture of the native English. As a proof of this, you will find in many parts of England (especially Shropshire) shafts and fragments of these crosses that evidently stood in the churchyard before the coming of the Normans used in the fabric of the restored edifice as though not only to destroy them but also hide them.

The idea travelled simultaneously into Scotland, Ireland, Wales, the Isle of Man, and Cornwall, who each according to their lights developed the art of the high cross.[1] It is even hard to compare them. Perhaps the Scottish examples are the most chaste and the Irish ones the richest and biggest, while the Manx crosses excel in their development of pictorial story-telling. The Cornish examples are small but very distinctive. One would have expected the Welsh ones to have had an affinity with either the Cornish, the Manx, or the crosses of the English Border. But they are not very like any of these. At the same time they give the impression of being inspired by a poor mimic rather than an original artistic genius.

What exactly was the purpose of any of these crosses is not known. Many of them bear commemorative inscriptions and most of them appear to have been erected within the sacred pale of a church. The great cross of Reculver was, in fact, erected within the church itself in a position later occupied by the rood screen. That is all that can be said. It is tempting to hold the theory that the original site of a church in pre-Saxon times was determined often by a standing stone which had marked a sacred spot in prehistoric times and still perpetuated the memory; that this rough pagan monument was replaced by one of the Anglian crosses, and that a church was then, or later, built adjacent to it. In a few places such a succession of monuments can still be seen. Thus, at Corwen, in the porch of the church, a prehistoric monolith remains standing upright though forming part of the fabric of the porch. Nearby is the remains of a large Anglian cross. At Rudston, in Yorkshire,

[1] Examples may be given among many others: Scotland, Ruthwell, Dumfriesshire; Ireland, Monasterboice and Kells; the Isle of Man, Maughold; Wales, Maen-achwyfan, Whitford, Flintshire (p. 41); Cornwall, Tintagel.

there is an enormous prehistoric monolith still standing in the churchyard.

Mr. W. G. Collingwood saw a distinct class in the Anglian crosses which have a rounded cylindrical shaft tapering into a square one. These he called "rood staff crosses," and believed that they originated in a carved wooden staff planted in the ground at a place where worshippers might foregather, and that, later, when the place became hallowed by custom, it was replaced by a stone monument larger in size but reminiscent in shape. The most perfect example of this type of cross is at Gosforth in Cumberland. Another, much larger, of which only the lower part of the shaft remains is in the churchyard at Wolverhampton.

Anglian Cross at Gosforth, West Side

Whatever their purpose in the beginning, these Anglian crosses were the forerunner of the mediaeval *churchyard cross* which was a particular object of hatred to the Reformers of the sixteenth century and is now, more often than not, only represented by a base. A few complete examples remain but they mostly belong to the late fifteenth and early sixteenth centuries.[1] Both the churchyard cross and the yew tree (if there is an ancient one) are on the south side of the church, and there may be some mysterious connection between them. After the Reformation, the churchwardens were fond of using the stump of the old cross as a stand for a sundial. But in times of plague, right down to the eighteenth

[1] As at Bitterley, Shropshire, and Derwen, Denbighshire.

century, the empty bases of churchyard crosses were still held in religious esteem by some communities. The sockets were filled with vinegar into which money was dipped to disinfect it. Some of these bases are still called *plague-stones*.

Perhaps the last churchyard cross ever to be erected between the Reformation and the Victorian church revival was put up in the churchyard of Ross-on-Wye, prompted by the ravages of a plague in 1637. In out-of-the-way places these churchyard crosses took on some of the attributes of the high cross in a market-town. That is, proclamations and other important public announcements were made from their steps. I can think of one typical though rather paradoxical instance—at Derwen, a remote place in the upper Vale of Clwyd. All public events were announced from this fine and undamaged cross in the old churchyard by the parish bell-man. These announcements included the dates and particulars about the next race-meetings in the neighbourhood, and I don't know that the parson who, no doubt, held forth from the pulpit on the sin of gambling, had any power to stop him. The incumbent does not seem always to have been master of his own churchyard cross. One remembers the Dartmoor vicar[1] who strongly objected to funeral parties carrying the corpse three times round the churchyard cross "against the sun." He suspected it as a superstitious rite. He could not stop it, however, by any means. In the end, he had to choose between condoning a pagan rite and perpetrating a desecration with his own hand. He chose the latter, and smashed his cross to smithereens.

The mediaeval preaching-cross, proper, was made by the friars. It differed in design from the other crosses by being combined with a pulpit. Only a single example of a friars' preaching cross is left in the country. It is at Hereford, standing in the grounds of the almshouses called Coningsby's Hospital. It is still on its original site adjacent to the ruin of the old Dominican friary.

Next to the churchyard cross the market cross is the most

[1] At Manaton.

numerous of our cross-relics, and architecturally it is the most highly developed of any. The right of holding a market in the early Middle Ages was a considerable privilege specially conceded by charter (either by the sovereign or lord of the manor). The market cross was therefore made a monument of importance and usually called the High Cross, whence comes that frequent name High Street. The market-place was the focus not only of the commercial activities of the town but also all the public affairs. And these matters were transacted at the high cross. From the steps of this proclamations were read. The court-house (moot-hall) stood in the market-place and judgments for whipping, pillorying, and putting in the stocks were carried out by the high cross. Although the common gallows were never in the market-place executions for treason (whether beheading or quartering) were carried out on a scaffold put up by the high cross. Likewise the burnings of heretics and witches. The most extraordinary case of this sort was the martyrdom of Bishop Ferrar of St. David's who was actually chained to the high cross itself, at Carmarthen. The men of the next generation mounted that part of the shaft against which Ferrar died as a pinnacle on top of the spire of Abergwili Church outside the Bishop's palace.

It is rare to find a market-cross older than the fourteenth century. Perhaps the most interesting exception is the high cross at Sandbach with its three great shafts of Saxon workmanship covered with carving. They were overthrown at the time when crosses were unpopular but later brought together again and re-erected. It is impossible to say whether there was a market-place there before or whether the three were planted as a wayside cross beside the highway to solicit the prayers of the passer-by like the Pillar of Eliseg in the Vale of Llangollen (a work of about the same date).

The fourteenth century saw a great restoration of market-crosses all over the country. In form they were like the new churchyard crosses of that date. That is, the shaft was set in a large square stone plinth with the top corners rounded or carved. Such is Neville's Cross outside Durham where the famous battle was fought. There is no market there now and this relic whose name has become a household word wherever English history is read is wedged into the wall of the garden of a little villa.

The steps were a feature of these crosses. They were used as stalls on market days. At Lydney and Clearwell in the Forest of Dean there are fine examples of eight-stepped crosses. Not many of the more ornate ones of this period are left, though Leighton Buzzard has an example, much restored and spoilt with modern figures. In it, however, one sees the beginnings of a sheltering canopy, a feature that was so much developed in the following century. The design was probably inspired by the Eleanor crosses which were made between the years 1291 and 1294. Two of them were not far from Leighton Buzzard. The Eleanor crosses are, of course, unique among our ancient monuments. There were originally twelve, each marking a halt of the funeral procession of Eleanor of Castile, wife of Edward the First, from Harby in Nottinghamshire, where she died, to Westminster Abbey. Three are left—at Northampton (73, 74), Geddington, and Waltham.

The canopied market-cross, which formed a shelter for privileged stallholders about the base of the cross came into vogue in the fifteenth century and was so popular that in several cases it was rebuilt in the seventeenth and eighteenth centuries after the cross itself had ceased to exist. Two well-known examples of this sort are the Yarn Market at Dunster and the Wymondham Cross. Of the mediaeval sort with elaborate stone canopies, there are examples at Salisbury, Malmesbury, Chichester (76), Shepton Mallet, and elsewhere. It is pleasant to remember that at Chichester the privileged stallholders were the poorer people. They were allowed not only to sell their wares here under cover but to do so toll-free. The Wymond-ham Cross is in two stories—an open arcaded ground-floor with a covered-in room above. But the Norwich Cross (now abolished) contained four shops and a chapel.

Boundaries of all sorts were marked out by crosses. Where private property was concerned the use of the sacred symbol was no doubt some insurance against the moving of the mark. On Dartmoor and on the great stretches of elevated moorland in the Cleveland District of Yorkshire many of the lonely crosses (46) whose use is unexplained may have been boundary stones. Some of them are placed in old tumuli of the Bronze Age at which so many early boundaries were fixed. These had no architectural pretensions like the boundaries of the religious houses. Many of the latter remain and among them are some of our most beautiful crosses of the plain sort. I have in mind one of the boundary crosses of the great Cistercian abbey of Vale Royal in Cheshire. This cross remains intact though the monastery itself has long ago been razed to the ground.

Wayside crosses set at cross-roads were no doubt our earliest signposts. In Devonshire, some of these are still in use as such, having had in more recent times the initial letter of places to which the four roads lead out on either face and at the end of either arm—I recall one near North Bovey on the fringe of Dartmoor. There are a few remains of "Calvary" crosses, that is crosses which have had an artificial hill built for them to stand on. The only instances I can remember having seen are at Lastingham in Yorkshire (a wayside Calvary) and Lincluden Abbey in Scotland. The mound called the "Dripping Pan" at Lewes is perhaps another.

The Monasteries

As ruins, the monasteries and the castles have one feature in common, they both suffered a deliberate act of abolition which reduced them to the state of roofless, floorless shells such as we are familiar with. The castles were "slighted" in the middle of the seventeenth century by order of the Commonwealth government lest the royalists should foregather in them again and make them centres of resistance. Most of them were rendered not only indefensible but uninhabitable.

The single sweeping blow from which the monasteries suffered fell a century earlier, when Parliament permitted Henry the Eighth to dissolve first the lesser then the greater monasteries so that all were empty by 1540. Afterwards, the agents of the crown were allowed to seize land, revenue, and treasures. This was a heavier and more far-reaching blow than the slighting of the castles, and yet, as a whole, the monastic relics which have come down to us are more numerous and perfect than those of the castles.

This long period of neglect has given both kinds of buildings a superficial resemblance in the eyes of our tourist and publicity organisations which class them in a single category, "old castles and abbeys." But that is not the spirit in which the serious sightseer should approach them for, as establishments, nothing could be further removed than the essentials of the castle and the monastery.

The castle is the soul of individualism. It perches itself on the most commanding site, is concerned only with the temporal security of its lord, and repels the stranger. In itself it is a work of engineering rather than architecture. Every castle, therefore, is an expression of the military possibilities of its site which is more or less highly developed according to the means at the disposal of its lord.

A monastery is the soul of altruism. It is the home of a community whose members work in this life to ensure security in the next. Its site is chosen for this purpose. The primary nature of its work is prayer and its workshop is therefore not a keep but a church. Another part of its work is to entertain strangers. In the mediaeval monastery the bulk of these strangers were pilgrims who came to visit the shrines of saints for which the monastic churches were famous. Owing to those things the monasteries tended to become architectural expressions of the communities and their works. The different orders had different views as to detail, but in all cases the plan was a uniform and not an individual one.

In order to understand the aims of the religious communities and the nature of their buildings one must take into account the following points.

In pre-Reformation times the Church was divided into clerics *secular* and *regular*. The seculars were the parish priests (or parsons) and the canons who served the secular cathedrals and collegiate churches. The regulars were hermits, monks, canons regular, and friars. Amongst these bodies there was a competitive spirit that has scarcely been surpassed by the feelings between Catholics, Protestants, and Nonconformists of our time. Although it is only with the regular clerics that we have to do here, we cannot keep the others out of mind.

THE MONASTIC ORDERS

A monk was a man who had taken the vows of poverty, chastity, and obedience, and had left the "outer world" to spend his life within the shelter of a convent precinct under a rule of conduct and thought. Since his novitiate days he might or might not have become a priest. The rule that he observed was that laid down in the sixth century by St. Benedict and the Order to which he belonged held a special view about the interpretation of that rule.

A canon regular was of necessity a priest; one who lived under a rule which was founded on the teachings of St. Augustine of Hippo. His interpretation of this rule varied slightly according to the order he belonged to which authorised that interpretation. The canons made a number of contacts with the world, serving the churches attached to their convent.

The friar was a preacher. He had his headquarters at a friary but his sphere of work lay entirely in the outer world.

A peculiar stumbling block for the uninitiated when trying to grasp the difference in outlook between the orders is the duplication of names. Thus it was Saint Benedict of Nursia who propounded the Benedictine rule, but Benedict of Aniane who, in the early tenth century, re-edited it. There are also two Augustines—both Saints. The one (usually styled *of Hippo*) who is credited with having propounded the canonical rule should not be confounded with the missioner who landed in Kent in 597.

The Benedictine rule had slackened off and been tightened up several times before the great monastic revival which originated at Cluny and produced the Cluniac order took place. In England hunting, hawking, and revels had crept into the monastic routine. There had even been married quarters in the monasteries.

Still, at its strictest, the Benedictine rule was a benign one. It did not look askance on art. It respected art as a manifestation of godliness in man and encouraged it in many forms. Cluniac opinion did not differ in this particular. But in the rule of the first Benedict much stress was laid on manual labour. Under the Cluniac régime the time for this was very much curtailed—almost done away with—so that longer services could be held.

The next important reformation took place in the twelfth century. This was of an entirely sweeping kind, comparable only to the Protestant outbursts of a later date—though it took place strictly within the fold of the Roman Church. The movement began in France, though the credit for its first impetus should belong to this country. A young monk of the Benedictine Abbey of Sherborne in Dorset, Stephen Harding, having made a journey to Rome paused on his way back at the Abbey of Molesme. Here he found the brethren very easy-going, but the Abbot and Prior so much of his own way of thinking on the subject of reform, that he was presently able to prevail on them to leave the monastery with a small number of kindred spirits and go off into the wilds to shape a rule of life nearer to the strictest interpretation of the first Benedict. The new monastery was founded at Citeaux. Robert, the Abbot, was compelled by the Pope to return to Molesme, so the Prior ruled the new model convent at Citeaux for a while, as Abbot, then, dying, left it to the original moving spirit, Stephen Harding.

So frugal and so unblest by wealth and circumstances were these monks that they had already become a laughing stock—when a real miracle happened. A party appeared outside the gates led by a young nobleman called Bernard. It was a reinforcement!—and the prestige of Citeaux was suddenly established. But things did not remain long as they were. Bernard was for advancing the cause of reform by founding another stronghold of the new asceticism. And presently he himself, as abbot-designate, and twelve zealots, representing in number Christ and His apostles, having received a small cross from Stephen, walked forth into the tangled forests of the Upper Seine. They proceeded for ninety miles, guided only by the lodestone of faith. The spot arrived at, rather than chosen, is described in the *Acta Sanctorum* as "a deep valley opening to the East. Thick, umbrageous forests gave it a character of gloom and wildness; but a gushing stream of limpid water which ran through it was sufficient to redeem every disadvantage."

Here they erected a building as simple as the shed at Bethlehem, and so established the monastery of La Ferté. Only after the most fearful privations, during which Bernard withstood with amazing constancy the pleas of his ragged and starved followers to return to Citeaux, did they survive the first winter. With the spring, consolidation followed conquest. In the ensuing year (1114) two new monasteries were established at Pontigny and Morimond, and at Clairvaux in 1115, St. Bernard remaining at this house till his death. By now the new movement had attracted a large influx of novices and became recognised as a new order of Benedictines, taking its name *Cistercian* from Stephen's house at Citeaux.

Bernard was a man of uncompromising stuff like all great puritans. As to art, he had no more use for it than John Knox, Calvin, or Luther. In the very phrases which they would presently use he cries out against the "strange designs which, while they attract the eyes of the worshipper, hinder the soul's devotion. . . . But as a monk, I say, Tell me, ye professors of poverty, what does gold do in a holy place? for we who have gone out amongst the people, who have forsaken whatever things are fair and costly for Christ's sake; who have regarded all things beautiful to the eye, soft to hear, agreeable to the smell, sweet to the taste, pleasant to the touch, all things which can gratify the body, as dross and dung, that we might gain Christ, of whom among us, I ask, can devotion be excited by such means? . . . By the sight of wonderful and costly vanities men are prompted to give rather than pray. . . . What has all this to do with monks, with professors of poverty, with men of spiritual

78 Remains of the Choir and South Transept, Netley Abbey, Hampshire

80   The Transitional Nave of

79   The rich Norman walling of the Lady Chapel

minds? In the cloisters what is the meaning of those ridiculous monsters, of that deformed beauty, that beautiful deformity, before the eyes of the brethren when reading? . . . Good God! if we are not ashamed of these absurdities why do we not grieve at the cost of them?'

So all kinds of restrictions were laid on the building of the new churches. There were to be no high towers, an embargo on bells, no carved ornament, altars to be painted in one colour only, candlesticks of iron, censers of copper, wooden crucifixes, habits of undyed wool and no silk to be used in vestments. In the letter these observances were preserved, and they created effects which the puritan outlook could never have foreseen. For although true simplicity was early abandoned after the death of the Cistercian Fathers, the flourishes of architecture in Cistercian buildings which grew richer with the ages were forced into a restraint that gave them a more perfect form than anything devised by the Benedictines. In fact the great Benedictine cathedral-abbey of Durham paid the Cistercian house at Fountains the compliment of copying its most vital development in the thirteenth century (p. 101). The prototype chapel of the nine altars (frontispiece), is hopelessly ruined, but the imitation at Durham is perhaps the most striking product of all our Gothic architecture.

The new *coda* had once more magnified St. Benedict's theory of manual labour, at which the Cluniacs had looked somewhat askance. This, coupled with the original ideal of the founders that the monasteries should only receive gifts in land and not in money, pointed to the fact that they must be self-supporting and live off the land which was given them. Hence they aimed at being agriculturalists, woodsmen, sheep-farmers, and horse-breeders. Unlike any other order, the Cistercians incorporated in each community a number of lay-brothers instead of paid servants to do the heavier manual work on their lands. These lived in separate quarters. They took the vows but remained unlearned and could not enter the priesthood.

Great ideas seldom appear singly in the world. Important brain-waves and soul-stirrings are nearly always

13

things of dual impulse. And the Cistercians were not alone in promoting their spiritual revival. While Stephen Harding was labouring to propagate his ideas in Burgundy, a similar spirit was abroad at the Monastery of Savigny in Normandy. This order of short-lived independence is known as Savigniac. The Norman connection with England was a vital one and the Savigniacs were soon founding houses in this country. But in 1148, on the invitation of St. Bernard of Clairvaux, thirty Savigniac communities in England turned Cistercian. These included Byland, Rievaulx, Buildwas and Furness. Such an important union so smoothly arranged is a striking testimony to the success of the régime and to the force of Bernard's personality.

The houses of the canons are counted among the monasteries, as they closely resemble the houses of the monks in plan and appointments. The canons, too, lived under a rule, but their orders may perhaps be described as semi-monastic. A contemporary observer[1] makes the following remark—"Augustine's Rule is more courteous than Benedict's. Among them, one is well shod, well clothed, well fed. They go out when they like, mix with the world, and talk at table." There was a "revival" among the Augustinian canons about the same time as that which took place among the Benedictines, though not by any means of so sweeping a character. The new order was founded by St. Norbert at his monastery of Premontré, near Laon. The order, called after the founder's house, received the unwieldy style of Premonstratensian. Its inception is dated 1120.

There is a rough parallel between the Black Monks (Benedictines) and the Black Canons (Augustinian), and between the White Monks (Cistercian) and the White Canons (Premonstratensian). In both cases whiteness stands not only for a colour in dress but also for a striving after a greater purity in principle and practice. And there was a further kinship. The situations chosen by the Premonstratensians—when they had a free choice in the matter—were precisely similar to those chosen by the

[1] Guyot de Provins.

Cistercians. And perhaps it is not irrelevant to remember that St. Norbet and St. Bernard were personal friends.

In matters of architecture the Benedictines spared no pains to make the most of the enrichments afforded by each successive style of architecture. The great Norman pillars of Durham nave are enlivened by a most elaborate and yet effective scheme of carved pattern-work. The natural austerities of Early English did not admit of much decorative flourish except carved capitals and brackets and insertions of polished shafts of Purbeck marble. The ornament called ball-flower came in with the Decorated style. Nobody took such advantage of this as the Benedictine monks of Gloucester. Its encrustment round the windows dazzles the beholder. The diaper is used as richly in the spandrels of the nave at Westminster. A novelty of the Perpendicular Period was stone panelling. No one took such advantage of this as the Benedictine monks—especially at Sherborne. In groining, in window-tracery, the Benedictines explored every possibility of splendour to the verge of extravagance. And they were wonderful connoisseurs of the grotesque.

While the Cistercians built in the Norman style they were nearer to their first ideal. The work is of the plainest. Its austerity is well seen at Buildwas where the period is so late as to include the pointed arch (81)—it was at a time when Benedictine Glastonbury was lacing every opening with elaborate raised chevrons. In the mid- and late thirteenth century, when you might have capitals well and inspiringly carved with stiff liliaceous foliage (p. 102) or peering heads or crouching beasts, the Cistercians stuck to their tenet in the matter of not allowing the likeness of anything in Heaven or Earth or the Waters under the Earth to be carved there. Instead, they built up even more refined and elevating effects out of studied adjustments and balances of simple mouldings. And such moulded capitals as may be seen at Tintern and the choir of Rievaulx are probably unequalled in refinement of expression. But the Cistercians in Wales could not resist carving their capitals.

As the Cistercians were missioners and pioneers they were

generally free to choose their own situation. In this they would be governed by two factors, a central site in the midst of the wild area that they were about to bring under cultivation, abundant water to drive the mill, fill the fish ponds, and flush the drains, a wood near at hand for fuel, and a flat stretch of sheltered pasture for the sheep to winter on. No doubt the story of St. Bernard's choice of site at La Ferté was in the minds of the settlers as a pious ideal—"deep valley, thick umbrageous forest, gushing, limpid water." At any rate there is a wonderful uniformity about the placing of the Cistercian monasteries, no matter what the character of the surrounding country. At Mellifont in Ireland, at Vale Royal in the Cheshire Plain, at Valle Crucis in the Welsh mountains, and at Rievaulx in the Yorkshire moors (85), there is the same feeling about the place, the identical "atmosphere." What the brethren made nearly perfect by the toil of their lives was, later on, rendered quite perfect (aesthetically) by the ruin of their house—the paradox is as strange as St. Paul's analogy of death and immortality.

THE REMAINS

The ruins of the monasteries are left to us in three forms, those which are still partly in use as religious buildings, those which are partly in use as secular buildings, and those which are wholly ruinous and open in every part to the sightseer, with his hat on or off (according to his personal sense of reverence). The variations are numerous. Carlisle, Canterbury, Durham, Ely, Norwich, Rochester, Winchester, and Worcester—all Benedictine except Carlisle which was Augustinian—were changed at the Reformation from cathedral priories into cathedral *colleges*, meaning a college of priests and not a school. New cathedrals were made out of old abbeys at Chester, Gloucester, Peterborough, Westminster, Bristol, and Oxford—the last two being Augustinian, and the rest Benedictine. The bishopric of Westminster only lasted for ten years, but the rest have continued. At St. Albans, Sherborne, Tewkesbury, and elsewhere the conventual church was acquired by the

The Design of the Nave Arcade, Tintern Abbey

[Edmund Sharpe del·

town to act as a parish church. In all these cases the monastic church has remained in continual religious use while the domestic buildings have been variously disposed of; in two cases, at Sherborne and Westminster, they have housed public schools.

At Bolton Abbey, Dunstable, Malmesbury, Lanercost, Shrewsbury, Waltham, and elsewhere the great churches have been less fortunate, only parts of them having been retained as parish churches while the rest fell to ruin. At the great Cistercian abbey of Beaulieu all was let go except the monks' dining-room which was converted into the parish church. Its pulpit, made to deliver the lighter forms of religious reading at meal-times, remained as an emplacement for the devastating homilies of the eighteenth century. At Much Wenlock the ruined church is open to sightseers, while the domestic buildings are in the use of a private occupier. At Cleeve Abbey the domestic buildings, though ruinous, remain wonderfully intact, while the church has completely disappeared. At Margam the nave of the conventual church serves the tiny village, but its chancel and the domestic buildings are all within the private domain of the great "castle" which has sprung from its ruins and part of the monastic buildings is converted into an orangery. At Bromfield, in Shropshire, the new owner incorporated the most sacred part of the church into his private house, and his bedroom windows are still to be seen in the chancel. But the most peculiar transformation of all is seen at Abbey Cwm Hir in Radnorshire. From here a whole arcade (five bays) of the monastic church has been transported lock, stock and barrel, carried over the wild hills, and set down thirteen miles away in the little town of Llanidloes, Montgomeryshire, for use as a parish church—a feat of engineering scarcely equalled by the Americans in our time.

In all this upheaval the Benedictine buildings did not fare so badly, for they were mostly situated in places where their use could be perpetuated in some form or another. But the magnificent buildings of the Cistercians which had been placed by design far from the centres and routes of humanity were simply stripped of lead and timber and left to rot. It is therefore such buildings as Tintern (90) and Rievaulx (85, 86) which have called forth the liveliest exclamations from poets and romantic writers, because of their contrasts of splendour and neglect. Before passing on to mention these buildings individually I will give a brief sketch of the lay-out of a monastery for the benefit of the sightseer, who may be unused to finding his way about such precincts.

THE PARTS OF A MONASTERY

The home of the monk was the cloister but his *workshop* was the church. In one sense, the cloister was a workshop, too, as the copying of manuscripts and the great business of the writing, illuminating, and binding of books was done there. But, as the principal *work* of the monk and the ecclesiastic was to serve God continually with prayer and praise, one must regard the church as the be-all and end-all of the monastery. So that perhaps the first impression (always a matter of practical importance in sightseeing) should be had here.

The monastic church (except in certain cases where the town had rights in the western end of the nave) was not a public building. It was intended entirely for use by the community and there was no "congregation" in the modern sense. Another point to bear in mind is that the word *choir* (the guide-books have returned to the older spelling of *quire*) has a different sense according to use. Structurally, an ordinary monastic church is divided as follows. The main body in the west is called the nave, the main body in the east the choir, while the cross-arms are known as the north and south transepts. The open junction of these four members is called the crossing. In a Cistercian monastery the community was divided into two bodies, the monks of the choir and the lay brothers or *conversi* who were purely agricultural workers, and were not expected to be learned or allowed to proceed to holy orders. They occupied the western range in the domestic buildings, used the western walk of the cloister, and attended service in the western part of the church, known as the lay brothers' choir. The other monks occupied the remainder of the domestic buildings, the three other walks of the cloister, and all that part of the church eastward of the space given up to the lay brothers which was known as the monks' choir. But the divisions of "monks' choir" and "lay brothers' choir" do not correspond with the main structural compartments of choir and nave. The monks' choir is usually carried down into the nave. It was terminated by a screen called the *pulpitum*, westward of which there was a space—usually the breadth of one bay—after which the rood-loft and its screen were carried across the church. But although the lay brothers were allowed a choir of their own, it is made ingenuously plain that it was the other which really mattered, for the "upper" members of the community were known simply by the style of monks of *the* choir. Perhaps this helped to brew the inferiority complex which cost the Cistercians the loss of their useful "lower" members in the latter part of the fourteenth century.

The cloister was generally placed on the south side of the church for the sake of warmth and light from the sun, though there are many exceptions. The eastern walk is usually backed by a building which has an upper story built upon a vaulted stone floor. In the lower part, adjoining the church, comes first the sacristy and the book-cupboard and then the chapter-house. The chapter-house being the pivot of the administration and discipline of the community is generally individual in its architectural appointments, and as it probably witnessed the most vital and moving scenes in the history of the community it is a place to pause in and let the mind "run on."

The chapter-house is usually followed by the monks' parlour where the rule of silence and that strictness of demeanour insisted on in church and cloister might be relaxed. Then comes the *slype* or passage leading to the infirmary buildings and to the monks' cemetery. This was the ever-apparent narrow way which every man knew he must take in the end to escape from the hard business of earning the favour of God to the reward for which he had

82 St. William's Shrine in the Cloisters,
Rievaulx Abbey

81   The Nave arcade and crossing:
Buildwas Abbey, Shropshire

83   Looking to the Eastern Chapel

84   The Abbot's Bridge

FOUNTAINS ABBEY, YORKSHIRE

toiled so assiduously. Perhaps nothing about a monastery rules the imagination so powerfully as the little portal and passage of the slype.

On the upper floor is the monks' dormitory, for which the old English form of *dorter* is now more generally used. It is approached from the cloister by the day-stairs, and a direct

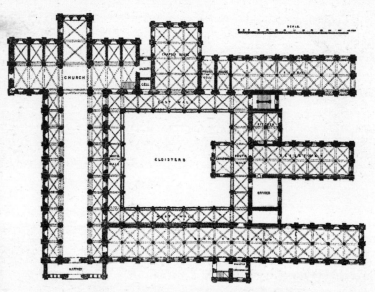

Plan of typical Cistercian Abbey

[Edmund Sharpe del

way into the church leads out of it called the night-stairs. At the other end it communicates with the *reredorter* (latrine). The principal building adjoining the side of the cloister opposite the church is the monks' refectory or dining-room— the guide-books have returned to the old English form of *frater*. In the Cistercian plan, where the whole of the western range was occupied by the quarters of the lay brethren, space was economised by placing the long refectory at right angles to the cloister. The kitchen is found beside it, while on the other side, or below it, is the warming-room, for warmth was considered a worldly

luxury not to be indulged in in church or chapter or at
work.

Behind the west walk of the cloister (and extending
beyond it) the cellarer had his quarters. He was lodged
here in the houses of all orders. In the Cistercian monasteries the lay brothers had their separate kitchen, frater,
dorter, and reredorter also in the western range, and came
directly under the authority of the cellarer.

The placing of the other chief buildings, infirmary, guest-
house, and the lodgings of abbot and prior varied a great
deal in different places. The most extensive of these was the
infirmary (called also the *farmery*). It was composed of a
large nave-like hall in which the sick-bays were placed, a
separate chapel refectory (the *misericorde*) and kitchen and
a lodging for the infirmarian. Sometimes, as at Rievaulx,
it has a separate cloister. Besides being used for the sick,
the infirmary was regularly occupied by the aged who had
grown too weak to bear the burden of the ordinary routine,
and also by those who were taking the three days con-
valescence and rest which was allowed for the periodical
blood-letting, an operation performed at quite frequent
intervals as a regular routine.

If you were to plan an expedition with the avowed object
of making an introductory acquaintance of the remains of
our monasteries I would say without a second's hesitation
that you ought to make, first of all, for Fountains, adjacent
to Ripon (1, 80, 83, 84), in the West Riding of Yorkshire.
It is incomparably the grandest and most complete *ruin* of
an abbey which we possess. In passing, I must urge that
you ought not to allow yourself, for the sake of any motor,
to be transported to the easiest access, which is at the west
end of the building. You should approach it (though it cost
you a mile and a half of walking) through the deer park.
There is no other vista in England so challenging to the
emotion and yet so simple in components as this one. A
broad interval of grass recedes between two banks which,
although they stretch away in a formal parallel are of
Nature's making. The right hand one is an escarpment of
yellow sandstone heavily embowered with enormous beech

85 Rievaulx Abbey, Yorkshire, looking on the Choir
from "The Terrace"

86 Rievaulx Abbey, the thirteenth-century Choir
from its south aisle

trees. Below the bank on the left runs the river. The ruin of the abbey, in colour, a luminous dun flecked with gold, fills the distance.

The disaster of the Black Death in the mid-fourteenth century set an economic problem which was largely responsible for robbing the Cistercians of their lay brethren, with a consequence that the western range in nearly all our Cistercian ruins is found to be either non-existent or very incomplete. But at Fountains it stands in entirety.

THE PRINCIPAL NATIONAL MONUMENTS

The National Trust has acquired no monastic buildings but it owns more than one priest's house. I have in mind that very interesting little fourteenth-century house which belonged to the parish priest of Muchelney. It stands just over the way from the farm attached to Muchelney Abbey, a Benedictine house now in the custody of the Office of Works. I have not been there since the Department took over. But I remember that the farmhouse was made out of the abbot's lodging, and that linen-fold panelling was still to be seen there. I also remember that the cloister garth was an orchard, while in the cloister walks stood huge butts of cider, and that the place seemed to have attracted to itself a sort of refined essence of the stillness that brooded over Sedgemoor on that summer afternoon. The silence was so ghostly that you could hear voices out of the past.

Of the other Benedictine establishments under the care of the Office of Works perhaps the most interesting is Tynemouth priory, a cell (i.e. affiliation) of St. Alban's Abbey. It stands on a splendid headland of yellow sandstone at the mouth of the Tyne. It is a fortified monastery, having been granted a licence "to crenellate" in the time of Edward I. Its castle gatehouse is still a very imposing building (now used as for army purposes) and what remains of its precinct walls are of the strong military type. The religious buildings are terribly ruined. The domestic ranges are razed to the foundations. But two splendid fragments remain of the church, the stone rood-screen and the east end wall, from floor to roof. This magnificent

PLATE 5.

TRANSITIONAL PERIOD

The Lay Brothers' Hall (*Domus Conversorum*), Quarters, Furness Abbey

[*Edmund Sharpe del*

piece of Early English work is a monument in itself. The sunlight plays on it, bringing out the rich golden colour of its stone and the shadow contrasts of its mouldings; and the sea plunges below the cliffs and touches it with the echoes of a chant of fate. But the beauty of the building and the

Tynemouth Priory, early thirteenth-century carved
capitals at the east end

grandeur of its situation made no appeal to the monk who had been sent down from the parent abbey. He wrote thus to his friend at St. Albans—"Day and night the waves break and roar, thick sea frets roll in, wrapping everything in gloom. Dim eyes, hoarse voices, sore throats are the consequences. Spring and summer never come here. The north wind is always blowing and it brings with it cold and snow or storms of wind. No ring-dove or nightingale is here, only the grey birds whose screaming denotes a storm. See to it, brother, that you do not come to so comfortless a place."

In a similar situation, though farther from the sound of the sea, stands Whitby Abbey on the Yorkshire coast.

The Chapel of the Nine Altars, Durham Cathedral,
derived from that at Fountains

[*Gerald Horsley del*

87 Glastonbury Abbey, Somerset
The scanty remains of the Nave, looking to the Transepts and
Choir, with the Norman Lady Chapel behind

88 Byland Abbey, Yorkshire

89 Llanthony Priory in the valley of the Honddhu, Monmouthshire

90 Tintern Abbey in the Wye Valley, Monmouthshire

Here, too, the domestic buildings are all gone, but the remains of the church are much more considerable than those of Tynemouth. The early history of the abbey is bound up with the fortunes of the Percies. Considerable remains of the pre-Norman monastery were found here during excavations, but these have been covered in again and turfed over.

Holy Island off the upper Northumbrian coast (60) is the Lindisfarne of Bede's writings, of which his hero St. Cuthbert was bishop in the seventh century. St. Aidan was here, too, and from here issued one of our principal national treasures, the Lindisfarne Gospel. Some remains of a pre-Norman monastery, but not as early as the Celtic Church, are to be seen. The priory was a cell of Durham, and the family link is reflected by the carving on the pillars of the church, which is a beautiful piece of Norman work wrought in red sandstone. The museum contains a unique collection of pre-Conquest gravestones and a number of crosses and carved slabs of the same period. Notable among them is one of a procession of warriors.

Another cell of Durham is Finchale Priory. Here, too, is a tentative reproduction of the carved work on the pillars of the church at the mother abbey. But it is done in paint-work and not carving. The fragments that remain are still bright in colour. Another architectural feature is a capital in the north arcade of the choir. Its treatment in carving is extraordinarily bold and yet so delicate. I fancy it must be unique. The mullion sill of the prior's study affords a striking piece of evidence that superstition will generate spontaneously. This entirely utilitarian piece of stone was easily accessible from the debris-cumbered ground before the Office of Works took charge. And it was the custom for female visitors to the ruin who desired the birth of an heir to stand on the prior's window-sill and genuflect so that the palm of one hand touched the stone in which posture the wish was made. The outlines of a foot and a hand graven on the stone indicates the orthodox points of contact. Is this sheer nonsense or a folk-memory of sanctity? The position of Finchale, at the wooded bend of a rushing river would have done credit to the genius of a Cistercian prospector, and it is satisfactory to know that it was the choice of a most romantic and prominent master mariner of the eleventh century turned hermit—his stone coffin remains where it was laid.

Four Cluniac houses are in the guardianship of the Office of Works. Castle Acre is the grandest of these ruins but my memory of it is pre-war and dim. At Thetford, preservation work on the church is nearly complete. The other buildings remain heaped with debris and unexplored. An interesting feature to be seen both here and at Castle Acre is the sacristy which is on the north, instead of the south, side of the church and contains a small oven for the baking of unleavened bread to provide wafers for the Eucharist.

The Cistercian houses under the care of the Office of Works total nine. Of these Tintern (90) and Rievaulx (generally accorded a French pronounciation, though the local people call it *Rivis*, a happy Anglicisation when given the peculiar Yorkshire *i*) are the most complete. The site of Rievaulx abbey is one of almost unparalleled beauty and, although the influx of modern pilgrims into that valley is enormous, the little village remains quite unspoilt, a thing for which we cannot be too thankful. The glory of Rievaulx is its great Early English choir (86). The walls of the aisles are fallen, so that the main arcades bearing above them the open arches of the triforium, crowned in turn by the openings of the clerestory windows, rise in their beauty of white-buff limestone through the natural tracery of the trees with a sublime ascension.

Owing to the nature of the site, the church is purposely mis-orientated, lying south and north, instead of east and west (85). The fine chapter-house, which shares with Norwich, Durham, and Shrewsbury the peculiarity of being rounded off in an apse, has at its entrance the unique addition of a shrine (that of St. William, first abbot of Rievaulx (82), the only disappointing thing about this magnificent ruin is the paucity of the remains of the quarters of the lay brothers.

Over the moors to the west lies Byland Abbey (88), a

91   The West Front

92   The North Nave Arcade, looking east
Llanthony Priory, in private ownership, accessible to the public,
but not treated by the Office of Works

94   The Norman Chapter-house, Buildwas Abbey

93   The Chapter House Entrance

walk of about three miles through an ancient deer park. The earnest pilgrim to Rievaulx should go to Byland first, and there leave wheels behind, and take to the path over the moors and through the deer park, so that that triple tier of arches I have noted may grow gradually on his consciousness out of the depth of the valley.

Except for a saving background, Byland has none of the beauty of position common to Cistercian abbeys, of which

Tile Paving in the South Transept, Byland Abbey

[*Brian Cook del*]

Rievaulx has full measure. But the pioneers were unusually restricted in their choice of site. They were Savigniacs from Furness Abbey who had first of all set out to found a missionary nucleus near the Scottish Border in 1134. But the Scots burnt them out. The obvious plan was to return to the parent community. But the abbot showed a very un-Savigniac spirit and was unwilling to give up his newly acquired rank. So they set forth again with uncertain aim, and after various vicissitudes settled near Thirsk. Here, after a short sojourn, the site proved too small. They were then given land in Rievaulx valley, over the water from the new abbey. This was intolerable to the Cistercians. To have one's chosen wilderness invaded, and that by a competitive order of reformers! They laid a complaint against the sound of the newcomers' bells. So the last move was naturally made in the makeshift spirit. On the new site there was neither a river nor good solid ground. The place was a marsh. It must have been a final and most bitter trial to them that in the same year their order was merged into that of the Cistercians. Nevertheless, they drained their marsh and built an abbey wall calculated to emulate that of their inhospitable rivals over the moor. It is a sad but very splendid ruin now (88) with little standing above the height of the ground story windows. A feature of archaeological interest here is the lay brothers' "lane." Both Byland and Rievaulx have the western porch to their churches (called sometimes Narthex or Galilee).

Although there is much less to see at Furness than at Rievaulx the ruin is even more imposing. Red sandstone buildings are often unpleasing in effect. Furness is an exception. The colour of its stone adds greatly to the quality of its impressiveness. Although the hotel stands within the monastic precinct, and the railway goes through it, there is an innate grandeur about the monastic buildings and their setting that holds its own in spite of the puffing of trains, in spite of the clicking of the batteries of cameras, taking family groups posed on the stumps of the nave arcade, in spite of the popping of the motor mowing the floor of the chancel!

Buildwas, although it lies within the fringe of an industrial area, is beautifully situated, where the Severn hews a gap through the great Triassic barrier of North Shropshire. In its church you may see well the first stirrings of the transition from Norman to Early English (81, 94). I have not been there since it became a national monument, but I have heard that a Burnell chapel with interesting tombs of that family have been discovered. This abbey as well as Furness and Byland was of Savigniac origin, but was absorbed at the time as the others into the Cistercian Order.

Some buildings seem to possess a personality which is not dependant on their use or their architecture; they have power to repel you or put you in awe, while others put you at your ease. Netley seems to me definitely to belong to the last class. It is built of a shelly limestone of a yellow-grey colour. Not a great deal is left of it except the church (78). There is no sign of the western range. The stone bellcote on the gable of the south transept is an interesting relic, as the rule about having only one bell was one of the fundamental things in which the order differed from the others. But the housing for the bell is seldom seen. Here you can see where the rim of the bell, when its bearings became worn, rubbed the stone, and the hole by which the bell-rope was led into the church through the transept wall is plain enough. Dedication inscriptions on the bases of two of the columns at the crossing are also uncommon, one of them makes mention of King Henry III. There are many happy architectural touches, such as the decoration at the spring of the arch within the east window. The fish-pond is still filled with water, but it lies just outside the present boundary. Part of a stained glass window from the abbey showing some charming enigmatical drawings of birds is in the museum at Southampton.

MONASTERIES IN WALES

In Wales, the history of monasticism is a different one. In the fifth century it was the old Celtic form which flourished. It was based on the system of the British church which appeared in these islands at the time of the Roman Empire. What we now call the Roman Catholic system came later. It was introduced among the Saxons by Saint Augustine in the seventh century, and did not affect the British Church in Wales. West of the Border there was no Saxon monastic period, and the Roman orders were not introduced into Wales until some time after the Norman conquest of England. Yet the remains of Celtic monasteries, owing to the temporary nature of the buildings are almost non-existent. The most substantial trace that has been found is the recent discovery at Tintagel in Cornwall which is now being excavated by the Office of Works. This settlement was evidently a large and important one, and its excavation bids fair to fill an important gap in our knowledge of the Dark Ages. Indeed the whole of the headland appears to be covered with overgrown foundations of small buildings.

Very soon after the Battle of Hastings, Norman influence penetrated into Wales, and with it came the Roman Church. The Welsh naturally looked askance at the spiritual mission of the new conquerors in which ulterior motives were fairly plain. But the Cistercians won their confidence and many houses were founded by the Welsh princes themselves. The most substantial ruin of a Cistercian house of this kind, founded by a Welsh prince and occupied by native monks is Valle Crucis near Llangollen. Here one sees clearly that the austerity of the order was relaxed earlier than in England, for, in the twelfth and thirteenth century work the capitals are as freely decorated as in a Benedictine house, instead of being confined to horizontal mouldings.

The Office of Works are guardians for three Cistercian monasteries in Wales, Strata Florida, Basingwerk and Cymmer, with Tintern in Monmouthshire. Unfortunately, the most interesting of these (from a Welsh point of view) is also the most ruinous. I refer to Strata Florida. There is nothing of any importance left standing of it except part of the west wall of the church with its doorway. But even in this fragment one sees a reflection of the same spirit as at Valle Crucis—a charter of liberties for art. In fact there is no other doorway like it anywhere. It is round-headed in the Norman fashion and recessed in five orders. Each of these intervals, instead of being filled with the usual series of nook-shafts surmounted by capitals and then arch-moulds, have five continuous rolls. These rolls are crossed in a vertical direction by stone bands which have the effect of rays. They do not terminate within the arch but coil tendril-like on the outer face of the walls, finally blossoming into small *fleurs-de-lys*. While the band which emerges midway, overhead, from the door has the remains of what must have been an exceedingly fine finial devised in interlace.

The Department has done extensive work in clearing the foundations of the abbey and in bringing to light many superb capitals, grave-slabs, and other carved work. To realize how wild and lonely the situation of Strata Florida is you must penetrate into its background of hills. These mountains are not as high or as rugged as those in the north but they are wilder, lonelier, and more unknown than any others in the Principality. Yet the monastery was intimately concerned in Welsh history, and was in being when Giraldus Cambrensis made his tour with Archbishop Baldwin recruiting for the Crusades.

Basingwerk, on the banks of the Welsh Dee is small and the remains are slight. But it is one of those ruins which has been improved enormously by treatment. A curious survival here is the serving hatch in the frater which still keeps its wooden lintel. A very fine carved ivory was picked up a short while ago by the custodian from the green turf floor of the chapter-house. How it made its appearance without being dug for is a mystery. I hope it will be returned to its natural site.

Tintern is technically not in Wales, and it lies securely behind a country where Anglo-Norman influence became paramount as early as the eleventh century (p. 95, 4, 6, 90). The only suggestion of Celtic feeling that I have been able to discover is to be seen in three fishes which form an inter-laced trinity on a grave-slab in the nave, and a bracket of inter-twined monsters. In extent of ruin Tintern is comparable to Rievaulx and might even rival it in situation, but the massive scenery of wood and cliff and water of the Valley of the Wye has not that true charm of spirituality which overwhelms one in the vale of Rievaulx. Moreover, the cloister at Tintern is to the north, a cheerless arrangement in winter, but one which would give good shelter from the sou'-wester which roars from the sea up the Wye Valley. Actually there are three cloisters, for besides the principal one and that of the infirmary, there is a lay brothers' cloister, a refinement which even Fountains has not got. But the church is the principal feature. It is very complete and its proportions are more pleasing than those of Rievaulx. The Office of Works has re-roofed the south aisle. Until the beginning of the nineteenth century the church had retained its great stone pulpitum which bounded the monks' choir, and stretched across the nave at the first bay west of the crossing. This was done away with by the early Romantics at a time when their ideas of gothicism and landscape gardening were confused, for the screen interrupted the conventional vista down the arcades. But it is a place where one is still torn between the aesthetic and the scientific aspect. In the treatment of Tintern the student has gained enormously, but in the deprivation of its mantling of the wild trellis and tendril, it has lost more than most places, and while Rievaulx has managed to keep its seclusion in spite of the motors, that of Tintern is completely reft away.

Two other monasteries in Wales have recently been taken over by the Office of Works—one is St. Dogmael's, which is situated in a village called after it on the south bank of the Teify Estuary which leads up to the port of Cardigan. The house, which belonged to the order of Thiron, a small offshoot of the Benedictines, was founded from Chartres. The ruin is in a deplorably neglected state and much is expected of the transformation. The adjacent church has for long been the concentration point for all the inscribed and ogham stones in the district. The other ruin alluded to is Talley Abbey, near Llandilo in Carmarthenshire. It was a Premonstratension house. Little is left, however, except the tower, but its situation by two lakes in a valley is enchanting.

Cymmer Abbey has none of the richness of the other Welsh Cistercian foundations. It has the severe simplicity of the original plan for houses of the reformed order. Its church was aisleless, though a small aisle on the north side is now to be seen—an addition of later date. Nothing remains of the cloister except the foundations, but in the extreme simplicity of the buildings one may read the message of Bernard and Stephen Harding more clearly than elsewhere. While, as if by compensation, in contrast to the buildings so plain and simple, the scenery is on the scale of full-grown mountains and is larger and grander than the setting of any other monastery in South Britain, including the Augustinian abbey of Llanthony (89, 91, 92)—but that has a very special story and ought not to be dragged in for any comparison.

The Department holds only one other Premonstratension abbey, Easby; it is in Yorkshire, a little below the town of Richmond. It is situated at a bend of the swift, lustrous Swale where the old canons' weir can still be seen, though its waters now grind out electricity at an inconspicuous installation on the site of the abbey mill. The ruin, although it is a very fine one strikes no alarming note of admiration; rather, it gives itself to the stranger with a most winning gentleness. The colour of the stone is one of the enchantments of the pile, being of a mouse-grey that has aged itself on to a foundation of buff, while there is a quality of blue in it that just eludes the eye though it haunts the memory, and one could have wished that the new custodian's house had not been such a bad misfit.

Easby Abbey was founded by a constable of Richmond Castle, the ruin of which cuts such a grand figure on its cliff up the river. Its dedication is to St. Agatha, and as St. Agatha's Abbey it is generally known in history. The Premonstratensian canons were much given to hospitality, and St. Agatha's was famous in this respect; the frater, which was the seat of entertainment, bears out the report with its magnificence. Its great east window over the dais, and those on the south side are enriched by that peculiar (if Frenchified) refinement, the pierced cusp. In plan, the cloister lies south of the church with the dorter in the western range. On the north of the church is the large range of infirmary buildings. But hardly anything remains of the church itself. Adjoining the abbey is the parish church. It was served by the canons though it is much older than the monastery. In the chancel stands the cast of a fine Anglian cross. It replaces the true relic which is in the Victoria and Albert Museum, South Kensington—a very disgraceful exchange which ought to be put right.

Of the Augustinian houses, seven are national monuments. Lanercost Priory (like Bolton Abbey) has had the nave of its church preserved by that part being kept for use as a parish church. Only the chancel is in ruins and this, together with the remains of the domestic buildings of the priory, is now undergoing treatment by the Department. It stands in Cumberland on the right bank of the Eden which has the Roman Wall cresting the hill to the north while, above a thickly wooded ravine cleft in the hill to the south, rises the castle of Naworth, the home of the Dacres who were the chief patrons of the abbey, whose tombs lie in the ruined choir.

Edward the First and Queen Eleanor came here in 1280. How they were met at the priory gate, and how they presented a gift of silk which was laid upon the high altar, is described with much spirit in the *Chronicle of Lanercost*.[1] But the priory was in a very unenviable place after Edward's failure to settle affairs with Scotland, and it suffered the brunt of more than one Border raid.

Kirkham Priory lies in a paradise such as the Cistercians would have chosen. Haughmond, in Shropshire, is in an unusual situation on the side of a hill some way above a river, but the site is one of great beauty. A rare thing to see at this abbey is the chapter-house doorway (93). It is of Norman work, but, in the jambs between the shafts, niches have been carved in the fourteenth or fifteenth century without any disturbance of the architecture, and figures have been set in them which still remain very little damaged by time or vandal. Then there is the church of the first Augustinian community to settle in England—at Colchester. A very interesting relic it is—built of bricks from the old Roman town.

White canons of Premontré were usually happy in their choice of a site. Egglestone Abbey, in the gorge of the Tees, near Barnard's Castle has not a great deal to draw the visitor out of his way to see except the lie of its lawns beside a river which has a darkling, vivacious beauty.

One other order has not been mentioned, that of the Gilbertines. It was a system rather than an order, an attempt to combine in church worship a choir of nuns with a choir of canons. The canons were to be Augustinian, the

[1] There are, however, doubts about the authenticity of this work.

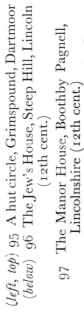

(*left, top*) 95 A hut circle, Grimspound, Dartmoor
(*below*) 96 The Jew's House, Steep Hill, Lincoln
(12th cent.)

97 The Manor House, Boothby Pagnell,
Lincolnshire (12th cent.)

98 Remains of the Norman house of the Constable of
Christchurch Castle, Hampshire

99 The vaulted undercroft, Boothby Pagnell Manor House

nuns Benedictine. The Office of Works preserves the relics of one Gilbertine priory at Mattersey in Nottingham-shire, but it is not one of the combined houses, being made for six canons only. It is very inaccessible and hopelessly ruined, so I cannot recommend it to the attentions of a sightseer who is not a keen archaeologist.

CHAPTER VII

The English House

(*From Saxon times to the Nineteenth Century*)

By Harry Batsford, hon. a.r.i.b.a.

(An asterisk (*) after the name of a house means that it is accessible to the public. To avoid disappointment, it should be understood that during wartime many of these houses and grounds are closed to the public.)

THE story of the English House is an oft-told tale, and its literature is still receiving additions. The books written on English domestic architecture would fill a decent-sized library, especially if the monographs on particular districts and single houses were included; they would cost a tidy penny, too, to acquire even if advantage were taken of reduced prices and the lower second-hand rates now ruling. There are many great folios, but, large or small, there are numbers with good text and illustrations recording sterling and attractive work, as well as a good deal of the shoddiest tripe ever brought forth. And yet it is a story never completed, to which it may be asserted justice will never be done, for no one has ever succeeded or ever will succeed in discovering all that there is to be known about the houses of some architectural significance in England, all their qualities and the many facets of their design and construction, the incidence and extent of their local types. They are still an incalculable number in spite of the ravages of fire and decay, crippling taxation, the callous and brutal sweeping away actuated by soulless commercial or bureaucratic busybodies, among other destructive agencies. To these has been added "the result of enemy action," but which, if more spectacular and catastrophic, has only carried on in more demoniac form the destruction wrought by mercenary native hands in a few decades. If Holland House and Crewe House have been burnt or blasted, they only follow in the train of Devonshire House, the Baroness Burdett-Coutts residence in Stratton Street, Chesterfield House, much of the Adelphi and a vast horde of historic places. Both agencies operate chiefly in large towns, and if the bomb is more rapid, the building—"improvement"—speculator is no less deadly. The Government has recognized this unhappy possibility, or prospect, of destruction and loss by setting up an organization for the collection, collation and carrying on of every kind of record of all buildings of historic interest, public or private. It is entitled the *National Buildings Record*, and Mr. Walter H. Godfrey, F.S.A., F.R.I.B.A., has been appointed Director. This work however arranged and however far carried out, will be of extreme value and importance not only for those old buildings which are destroyed but for those which survive. But it is too early yet to speak of the methods and effects of this projected plan.

English dwellings range from the enormous mansion, covering the area of a small village with its vast out-buildings, through the smaller country house, the large farmhouse, the cottage, the whole range of inns down to the smallest one-storey hovel. It may be a commonplace truism, but it is worth saying once again that they represent in the aggregate with their craftsmanship, exterior and interior, one of the most characteristic productions of the English race, enshrining some of its typical qualities—well-proportioned dignity, appropriateness to practical use, unpretentious and orderly charm. They also form one of the most considerable heritages, though unfortunately a distinctly perishable one; even if, as in this passing casual glance, we restrict ourselves mostly to buildings to which the public has regular access, they are too great in number and too diversified in type for any one volume to embrace. Many reviews in the past have been affected by two disorders: they have been in every age too concerned with the extremely large mansions erected by the exceptionally rich, or in the later centuries have been preoccupied with prominent architects and their productions, to the virtual exclusion of the pleasant and abundant vernacular house of anonymous workers; they have produced in effect a history of English architects rather than of houses. For, parallel with the movement initiated by the Quennells to visualise the fascinating interest of the life's work and play, prayer and quarrels of everyday folk, attention has during the present century been much more directed to their dwellings: the small country or town house, the farm and its accessories, the inn and the cottage. Mr. Addy also has probed the marked historical significance of quite humble little buildings in the North, nearly all of which have since been ruthlessly swept away.

Perhaps one of the pleasanter compensations afforded by the 1939 war to those evacuated to strange districts for work and dwelling has been the opportunity of making the fairly close acquaintance of a number of new historic houses: a high-lying stone hamlet, a great brick farmhouse and cluster of half-timber cottages down a wide green-margined side lane, a four-square Restoration guest-house, and a derelict Regency mansion, brooding behind the wide stretches of its mournful park.

For many of these home-exiles there will be pleasant memories of new associations, a few friendships even, the contact with country folk in town and village with their own deep-seated experience, their different outlook on past and present-day affairs. But if the human fellowship has failed, as it is always likely to do, and most people around seem hard, narrow, and grim, stolidly indifferent, or unwelcoming and inhospitable, mercenary and unserving, then there is an unfailing solace in having added diversely and substantially to one's friends among houses; they are always there when you call upon them; they are not in the least shy of displaying their excellences; free from all taint of snobbishness, they do not hide, if they do not flaunt, their commonplaces or defects. Their makers and dwellers have put into them their own qualities, just that sturdy English cheerful, matter-of-fact fitness which has enabled them to stand up to their job for a matter of some two to

116

five centuries, will keep them in the same quiet usefulness for as long again, and will see us, somehow, some time, through the present war.

It is a joy to have discovered one such house at the top end of the West Midlands. It is not even in a hamlet, yet it is not alone. It stands at the finish of a dead-end field track, on a little shelf, cut off by the river sweeping around, looking for ever across the plain to the Cotswold high line. It is a rambling gabled plaster and brick affair in which most of the seventeenth century had a hand. Substantial as it is, it is dwarfed by its mighty four-way brick dovecote in front on its separate knoll. Hard by is the tiny church where Norman craftsmen lavished their patterned luxuriance, but its short, though well proportioned tower may have been built by Dick Whittington, for it is said that hence he started on his memorable journey. When first visited the house was a *Church Wayfarers' Home*, though now apparently it is a temporary haven for evacuated schools; the writer hopes to end his days there, if the effects of war taxation, and what is worse, the appalling Hell-utopia of a frantic gimcrack New Order with which we are threatened after the peace, have done their work too thoroughly. But probably there will be no room for a wandering, broken business man?

Demagogues have inveighed against the uselessness of the large mansions which their crack-brained schemes of bureaucratic pauperisation have to the country's detriment caused to be abandoned by their original owners. This war has proved their abundant and varied usefulness: they have not failed to contribute their full quota of national war service. They have housed satisfactorily the exiled Government staffs, the Royalties even, of overrun kingdoms; they have accommodated great public schools, with some loss of convenience and efficiency, it must be confessed, till drastic agitation compelled the return to their own buildings commandeered by avid departments and allowed to lie waste. In the Welsh border country they have been turned to good account as girls' schools, and generally empty country houses have come in handy for storage of all sorts of useful commodities; in fact their uses have been as diversified as unexpected. One delightful elderly lady writes about one of the finest mentioned in these pages: "How are you standing up to these great days? My house is given over to a museum, different picture galleries, a day school, a dancing class, the R.A.S.C., some private property of a great glass collector and various other things. One of the curators has turned out very handy in the garden. What a life!"

It is hoped, probably with undue optimism, that this war will see out the extinction of an ensanguined class-consciousness in a united regard for the common weal. Let none assert that, whatever their uses, the country houses of England are not a definite national asset.

The Mediaeval House

There is a gap of seven hundred years in our recorded history during which time the human dwelling-house is not represented by any ancient monument, a space that can be compared exactly by looking back from the date of publication of this book to the year in which Edward I was born. In short, there is nothing to be seen between the Roman house and the Norman house unless we split hairs over the late Romano-British hut-circles (95) in Wales or Cornwall or the cells of early Christian monks of the Celtic persuasion.

Angles and Saxons, Danes and Norsemen evidently lived in wooden houses which have disappeared. When more durable materials are used again the house has become something very different from what it was in the days of the Roman villa. It is called an *aula*, from whence comes the more English word *hall*. This was a sort of general purpose building that was erected alike as a house of man and a house of God. There was, in fact, no practical distinction between the rich man's hall and the church. Both buildings consisted essentially of a nave and side-aisles. In each, one end was regarded as being more honourable than the other. If it were a church, the honourable portion was the east end which contained the altar and the space adjoining it, where the priest officiated. If it were a hall, the end contained the high table at which the lord and his family sat. That was called the *upper* end, and in order that there should be no mistake the floor was raised a matter of six inches or a foot to form a *dais*.

The only difference between the church and the hall was necessitated by the mortal nature of man as compared with the sublime material independence of the Spiritual Presence. When the earthly lord retired from his dais at the upper end of the hall, he was provided with a bed-sitting-room called a *solar*, while at the lower end of the hall there was also an appendage or two in the shape of kitchen and larder and possibly other "offices," such as bakehouse, brewhouse, and stables. When night descended on the establishment, the lord and his family went to bed in the solar or (in the larger houses) another private room called variously the *parlour* or *chamber*, while the whole of their retinue made up their shake-downs on the floor of the hall.

In the Norman castle it was only the relative position of these rooms which was altered. They were placed one on top of the other instead of end to end, the hall being on the first floor. The castle had certain amenities owing to the thickness of the walls in which it was possible to build small sleeping chambers for distinguished guests, and also latrines whose discharge could fall conveniently into a moat.

Although the castle was a wholly Norman importation into this country the hall was not. The Saxon thegns had lived in wooden halls. But there was a difference, for the Saxon halls were true bungalows, being ground floor buildings, whereas those of the Normans were raised one floor up. Although King Harold is seen feasting in a first-floor hall in the Bayeux tapestry, it will be borne in mind that this is a device of Norman needlework in which all Saxon details are unreliable.

There are several Norman houses surviving, at Southampton, Christchurch (98), Lincoln (96) and Bury St. Edmunds. Perhaps the best example is at Boothby Pagnell (97, 99). This is a manor house. But neither here nor in the other specimens—which are town houses—is the arrangement of the full-blown hall shown, as they are not aisled buildings. That is seen best at Oakham and Leicester, though these are castle halls and not self-contained houses.

One can gain a better idea of things as perpetuated in the thirteenth century, particularly at the old manor house of Stokesay, near Craven Arms, in Shropshire (100). This is actually called Stokesay *Castle*, for a strong tower with battlements was added in the following period and the place is surrounded by a moat and entered through a gatehouse. But it is essentially a manor house, and all the domestic arrangements, when it was a plain thirteenth century knight's hall, remain practically unaltered.

Many simpler houses of the fourteenth and fifteenth centuries, all built on the hall plan, remain, a number of them being half-timbered structures throughout, though it is common to find that the old hall which was built open from the ground to the roof has had an upper floor placed in it.

Some interesting specimens of the hall-house as used by the clergy survive. At Muchelney, in Somerset,* and at Alfriston, in Sussex* (102), a priest's house is preserved by the National Trust. These are ground floor halls. At Ruthin the old building of a college of priests attached to the church has been adapted as a modern rectory, and this, though a thirteenth century building, is on the Norman plan of a first-floor hall.

These examples of mediaeval houses up to and including the fourteenth century are individually interesting, but do not show any great advance in planning or design. Though there is a fair amount of diversity, there is a strong family likeness between them, with their contemporary window tracery. Naturally more stone have survived than of any other material, and they range from great rambling structures, frequently quadrangular, such as Penshurst in Kent,* and Broughton Castle, Oxfordshire* which have usually received extensive additions in succeeding centuries, to quite small manor houses, such as Charney Bassett and Sutton Courtney, both in Berkshire. The first is notable for the survival of the contemporary open hearth in the centre of the great hall. Little Wenham Hall, Suffolk, is an interesting two-storey example with one part carried up as a tower, and is remarkable for its early use of brick. In Lower Brockhampton Hall, near Bromyard, Herefordshire,

100 Stokesay Castle and Church, Shropshire, showing the great Hall and Keep

101 A fifteenth-century small house of yeoman type, Bignor

102 The fourteenth-century priest's house, Alfriston

EARLY SUSSEX HOUSES

there is the remarkable survival of a small fourteenth-century timber house with a fine roof in the hall, and a miniature fifteenth-century gatehouse, also in half timber.

Lower Brockhampton, Bromyard, Herefordshire
The fourteenth-century hall and fifteenth-century gatehouse
[*Sydney R. Jones del*

With the fifteenth century came greater differentiation and the use of local materials in design. East Anglia produced some excellent houses in brick, such as Giffard's Hall, Stoke-by-Nayland. The similarly named house near Wickhambrook is of timber; both these possess fine wood-panelled solars. Of these Tudor interiors, innocent of Renaissance influence, not many remain. Perhaps the finest of all is the Abbot's Parlour at Thame Park, with its linenfold panelling and upper range of large panels with mutilated roundels, where a touch of Renaissance detail prevails, which is not inharmonious by contrast. The

ceiling, comparatively plain, is divided into four by a
moulded beam with running ornament on the soffit and a
central pendant. Wolsey's closet at Hampton Court* is a
parallel but much smaller example where the definitely

Interior of the Hall, Lower Brockhampton

[*Sydney R. Jones del*]

Renaissance frieze and ornamental ceiling have a mixture
of lead.

To the eastern part of the country belongs the local
manifestation of enormously tall twin-towered gatehouses,
as seen at Oxburgh and the Deanery at Hadleigh. As with
house design in general, this type is carried over into the

sixteenth century, where we get the tallest of all at Layer Marney, of eight storeys, with its Renaissance detail in terra-cotta. A fair number of fine fifteenth-century houses survive, such as Little Sodbury Manor House, Ockwells Manor, Berkshire,* half timber and brick, with its great windows and fine glass; Cothay, Somerset, with its gatehouse, and the wool merchant's house of Great Chalfield, Wiltshire, grouping pleasantly with the little church hard by. Larger is Compton Wynyates, Warwickshire,* quadrangular and built of brick, with half timber gables; Ightham Mote in Kent* is a half timber and stone parallel. In none of these houses was there anything much in the way of an attempt at symmetrical planning or elevation design, though this development was close at hand.

Meanwhile the South-east had evolved a smaller type of yeoman's house with central hall. The centre is recessed between two projecting ends connected by curved braces (101, 104). These halls mostly run to two storey height before the beginning of the roof, but it has been pointed out that they are developed from an earlier type of hall which sprang from a lower single storey level, as at houses at St. Osyths, Little Dunmow, and Great Warley, Essex. Samples of these are particularly abundant in Kent, where at one time fifty houses of this kind were said to have been counted within a short distance of Maidstone. The type is seen at Pattenden, Goudhurst; Shorne; Synyards, Otham (104); with Stoneacre* immediately adjacent. In nearly every instance the inconvenience of the central hall, cutting the building into two parts, has caused it to be divided into two and floored over, frequently as early as 1550. Stoneacre, now owned by the National Trust, is an example in which the Central Hall has been opened up; it has, however, had portions of other houses tacked on to it.

Where the central hall survives, it is frequently remarkably impressive, as at Stoneacre, and still more at Great Dixter, Northiam. These fine roofs are comparable with Cothay, in Somerset, and Little Sodbury, already mentioned, and at Weare Gifford, in Devon, where the roof is of typical West Country luxuriance.

The prevalence and prosperity of the weavers' craft have left fine examples of the fifteenth century, which show there was a time when industrialisation and beauty went hand-in-hand instead of suffering a fundamental divorce. William Grevel's house at Chipping Campden is well known, as also is "Paycockes," Coggeshall,* with fine restored interiors, and the houses of such weaving village-towns as Lavenham in Suffolk, with Kersey not far away, where the houses are later in style and probably date from some time early in the sixteenth century.

At the same time, a fine wood-panelled solar with either a flat moulded beam or gabled open timber roof was developed, as at Giffard's Hall, Stoke-by-Nayland, Cothay and Great Dixter.

Little can be said about the hovels which, in the Middle Ages, sheltered the cottager. They were of flimsy timber construction probably filled in with wattle and daub, and none have survived. They could quite easily be taken down, and re-erected; in fact, it was one of the grievances of landowners that villeins in the later middle ages decamped from the manors to which their serf conditions tied them, and either took their houses with them or knocked them level with the ground. It is a curious fact that even in stone districts the peasant's cottage in the Middle Ages was not built of this substantial and enduring material. Mr. Addy has shown something of the development of such small structures towards the close of the Middle Ages, when extra chambers were incorporated, and in the North a byre for beasts, with sometime an upper storey reached by a ladder or steep ladder-like stair. Nevertheless, by the fifteenth century a type of half-timber cote had been evolved which must at least have offered some approach to comfort and convenience. This can be seen in the MSS of the later Middle Ages, largely of course of Flemish origin, though it is probable that the English cottages were not so very far behind them. The Grimani Breviary shows thatched half-timber cottages with small dormers, which would accord excellently with surviving examples of slightly later date, if set down in Worcestershire to-day. It would be extremely helpful if records could be made of cottage illustrations in MSS by such artists as Gerard David and Jean Foucquet, where they appear occasionally as part of the background of charming landscape scenes. It is curious that it was thought worth while sometime ago to devote a book to the textile backgrounds of some of the National Gallery paintings.

There is no space here to describe the remarkable early form of construction based on crucks or curved timbers, frequently massive, which were thought necessary to support the roof-beam. A curious example of the triangular-shape house thus obtained is to be seen in "Teapot Hall," near Scrivelsby, Lincolnshire, though its decrepit condition seems to show that this little structure of unique interest will not be with us much longer. But the crucks, owing to this misconception, were retained even when greater head-room was afforded by raising vertical side walls. This primitive cruck construction was usually found in the North and West, beyond a line crawn from the Severn to the Humber, and a number of examples can still be seen, e.g. as recorded in the Herefordshire volumes of the Historical Monuments Commission; it probably persisted as late as the seventeenth century. The forces of destruction, however, combine powerfully to abolish survivals by demolition, and it is unlikely that a great number will last beyond the next few decades.

The mediaeval illuminated manuscripts are a still richer source of examples of fine gabled timber town houses—in Flanders, of course, which are enough to make any interested person long for the reconstruction of a fifteenth century Flemish town. It is probable that such timber houses in England were neither as large, elaborate nor extensive, but Shrewsbury in some of its alleys can show a fair number of not unimpressive survivals, as in the case of Butcher Row, with its small but fine series of unspoilt mediaeval shop fronts. It is to be regretted that the reforming sanitary zeal of the citizens of Hereford swept away in the nineteenth century an even finer series of which only the well-known Butcher's Guildhall remains. The Hereford people also managed to abolish the finest and largest of John Abel's guildhalls, with its multiplicity of gables. Worcester can still show a number of these irregular projecting timber-gabled houses in such places as Friar Street and New Street, but both here and at Gloucester they seem to be in the last stages of decrepitude, and even if, as is locally suggested, the former town is anxious for their preservation, it is doubtful if, without drastic repair, they can manage to survive.

In the sixteenth century the English cottage, like the yeoman's house, came into its own, and fortunately there is an excellent variety of examples surviving, though not even the separate volume devoted to them in the "Heritage" series and the earlier monographs on different districts can be said to exhaust the subject. The South-Eastern group in half-timber, later weather-proofed by the insertion of brick fillings between the timbers, or by plastering, tile hanging and weather-boarding, is outstanding for the fine character of its design and the excellence of its craftsmanship (103). The Cotswold type found along the Oolite belt from Dorset to Lincolnshire, is equally distinctive and distinguished, especially of course in the hills of Gloucestershire. There is excellent East Anglian cottage design in various districts that is plastered over its timber, or weather-boarded in parts of Essex, such as the coastal areas. In the West Midlands, up to and over the Welsh Border, there is another, though less distinctive group of half-timber "black and white" structures, and mention must finally be made of the cob cottages of Devonshire, plastered and whitewashed, and the uncompromising massiveness of the North and of the granite-block structures of Cornwall. Few cottage interiors have remained unaltered, but the Priests' House, West Hoathly, Sussex* (103), illustrated as an unpretentious typical building, contains some reconstructed interiors filled with local furnishing in wood and metal (105). In the latter material there is Mr. John Everett's fine collection at Lewes, as well as Miss Jekyll's gift of cottage furnishings to Guildford Castle, and the group in the Museum at Brighton.

It is rather remarkable that although in private houses the hall returned to its Saxon location on the ground floor after the Norman period, it remained at first floor level in the line of descent which perpetuated it as a municipal building. The moot-hall was built like this right on into Georgian times, as may be seen at Keswick and in many a quaint example of the Elizabethan and Stuart periods such as the moot-halls of Appleby and Much Wenlock and the Market House at Ross-on-Wye, when the hall as a unit of domestic architecture was disappearing altogether.

When the Tudor period came, many of the great landowners, who would have built themselves castles at an earlier date, were raising great stone houses of the hall type. But evolution had already set in and both upper and lower ends were developing T-shaped wings at right-angles to the long main buildings. The main door was still at the lower end of the hall, opening into a passage with a door at the far end. Such an arrangement may still be seen in the halls of the colleges at Oxford and Cambridge. The passage is called the *screens*. It has on one side of it the hatches of the buttery (through which beer and wine are brought up from the cellar) and the pantry, with a passage leading from the kitchen in between. On the other side is an oak screen with two doors in it leading into the hall, while the roof of the passage forms the floor of the gallery which looks into the hall, sometimes called the musicians' gallery, though authority for this name seems to rest on romance. At the upper end of the hall, beyond the dais and its high table, the old chamber and solar have become magnified with the addition of *lodgings*, that is bedrooms for the family and guests, the extra rooms being provided in the T-shaped enlargement. An equivalent enlargement has been made for the feudal staff at the other end.

By this time additional light has been provided for the quality at the high table through an oriel window reaching from the floor to the eaves, as seen at Easby Hall, Hampton Court, Fawsley, Horham Hall, Essex and elsewhere. In some cases a large fireplace has been built to conduct the smoke away, instead of having the hall heated by the old-fashioned brazier in the middle of the floor whose fumes escaped through a louvre in the roof. The fireplace is an amenity but not an innovation, for the Norman Hall at Christchurch has one, and its tall chimney still stands (98).

THE HALF-TIMBERED HOUSE

This is a simple construction of wooden framing in which the blank spaces between the beams and uprights were filled in either with clay "daub" on a wattle foundation or brickwork ("nogging"). The districts which have the most numerous half-timbered houses to show are naturally those which are lacking in local supplies of stone—the downlands, the Eastern Counties, and the great red clay shires of Cheshire, Herefordshire, Worcestershire and Warwickshire. Cheshire owns the two finest examples of large half-timbered houses which have yet been put into preservation as National Monuments, namely Moreton Old Hall at Congleton* (109) and Rufford Old Hall near Ormskirk.* Both are properties of the National Trust. In Herefordshire, the village-towns of Ledbury (110) and Weobley are beautiful examples of the picturesqueness of this type of building. For a town of its size perhaps Tewkesbury in Gloucestershire has the greatest number of half-timbered houses surviving, including a good specimen of a fourteenth-century house, which is a rarity. In Kent, the National Trust have recently acquired nearly the whole of the small village of Chiddingstone* (108) which will ensure the preservation of a number of interesting little buildings of this kind that are rapidly disappearing all over the country under orders for demolition.

It was not only the lack of stone which promoted the building of the black-and-white house. It was popular in such towns as Sherborne, in Dorset where stone was plentiful, and in York, where it was easily obtainable by cheap water carriage. In such places wooden construction had distinct advantages over stone. Thus, if the site of your house was confined you could extend the width of the upper floors by bracketing out the first floor and making it overhang the pavement. Pedestrians found no fault with this until the days of top hats, as it tended to keep them dry

103   The Priest's House, West Hoathly, Sussex

104 Synyards, Otham, Kent, an early sixteenth-century house of
south-eastern type with later Dormer

105 The Priest's House, West Hoathly: an interior with
contemporary furniture

in wet weather—the top hat had a great deal to do with the first onslaught on these picturesque projections in the twelfth century. In Chester, a still more curious development of the half-timbered building is found. In that city the mediaeval houses were built with stone-vaulted basements whose floors at a remote date were on the level of the street but are now several feet below it. Owing, probably, to the impassable nature of the main thoroughfares, a footway was formed at first-floor level, the houses recovering the room they lost at that stage by over-hanging the walk with their second and superencumbent floors, forming what are called "rows" which still exist, the unique pride of the city.

The centuries principally represented are the sixteenth and seventeenth. Fifteenth-century examples (101) are comparatively rare, and fourteenth (102) very rare. No doubt great fires are more responsible for this than old age for wood lasts amazingly out of doors, as may be seen by the wooden church at Greenstead-juxta-Ongar made in the Saxon Period. Time after time one comes across the record of an accidental fire which rendered the greater part of a town's population houseless and, quite apart from this, the deliberate act of armies in the feudal and Cromwellian wars must have accounted for wholesale demolitions of the earlier types of our wooden and half-timbered houses.

THE RENAISSANCE

The new culture of classicism made itself felt in our architecture through four historical impulses. The first was the union of the House of Lancaster with that of York after the Battle of Bosworth in 1485 when Henry Tudor married the heiress of the House of York and put an end to the faction enmity of the Roses. The epoch was heralded with much church building and the founding of university colleges, in which renaissance forms began to insinuate themselves into the old Gothic models. Next came the accession of Henry VIII, who was a passionate apostle of the Italian and classical cults that were sweeping Europe. He had more money to spend than any sovereign since the time of Edward III, and he and his princely cardinal emulated each other in the building of colleges and palaces. Merchants of the wool staple and great subjects built themselves houses on a similar plan, which was that of the courtyard castle domesticated instead of embattled. Such palaces as Hampton Court and such houses as Hengrave (107), Layer Marney, of Compton Wynyates still bear witness to the scale of their builders' ideas.

You can trace the domestication of the courtyard castle from the well-defended Bodiam* (71) (1386) through Hurstmonceux (embattled, but built of brick, 1435). Kirby Muxloe (moated but scarcely embattled; of brick, 1480), and Oxburgh* (ditto, 1482). The plan is the same for manor-house or college, a picturesque compromise between the hall-house and the fortress, dovetailed by an interesting process of evolution. The various defensive elements, *machicoulis*, embattled parapet, loop-hole, turn themselves into decorative features like the mouse-trap in the story of Cinderella, while the garrison with its men-at-arms become a body of retainers that is more obsequious than soldierly. The formidable gatehouse becomes the picturesque entrance with a porter's lodge inside instead of a guardroom (and no dungeon below). When you pass through you see the entrance to the great hall immediately opposite you, across the quadrangle, with the oriel window to the right of it, indicating the position of the dais and the "upper end." Taking their cue from this, the more honourable buildings such as the chapel and superior lodgings will be on the right-hand side of the quadrangle and those associated with the domestic staff on the left.

By the third historical impulse mentioned above is meant the dissolution of the Monasteries (1539). Hundreds of valuable estates with the best type of stone buildings that could be converted to secular use or made quarries of, were thrown on to what was practically the open market, though of course the court favourites bought first, receiving their knock-down bargains as "presents" from the King.

The result of this ubiquitous swap of lands and building material from churchman to layman was not immediately

106 Burton Agnes Hall, Yorkshire

107 Hengrave Hall, Suffolk. The Entrance Front

108 Chiddingstone, Kent: a village preserved by the National Trust

109 The Courtyard, Moreton Old Hall, Cheshire, with
Richard Dale's famous bay windows

apparent. It took a decade for men to regain their breath and collect their thoughts. By that time another king was sinking into a decline and there was a prospect of Catholic Mary becoming queen. Who could tell what would then be done to the men who had cashed in on the fall of the monks?

In fact, it was not until Elizabeth came to the throne that the great resources of the empty monasteries began to be used. Then an absolute house-building mania flared up all over England and Wales; houses, houses, houses, and for a whole century hardly a new church was raised to the glory of God anywhere.

The Elizabethan house is a building to delight the artist and not the pure architect. And the artist only likes it because it has worn and weathered picturesquely, and fits in with sunflowers, hollyhocks, beehives, and box-hedges. The endless plaster-work over the fireplaces and on the ceilings (111) he admires, but it is their quaintness and not their beauty which wins him. When all the traditional standards of the aristocracy, the Church, and the trade guilds had been thrown overboard for a school of architecture invented by the ancient Greeks, debased by the Romans, re-used by the mediaeval Italians, and passed to us via Germany, Holland, and the Netherlands, to be copied on arrival by local craftsmen under the direction of gentlemen who were more concerned with a "conceit" than a style, the picturesque crudeness of our Elizabethan classicism is not to be wondered at.

The smaller Elizabethan house was an abridgement of the mixture which had produced the courtyard house. The built-up front containing the gatehouse disappeared and was replaced by an ordinary wall with a more or less elaborate gateway in the middle. The hall range, instead of being the base of a square became the cross-bar of a wide letter H, while the doorway took on some of the ancient grandeur which used to reside in the gatehouse, and was entered through a porch whose projection was often carried up through all floors to the roof-line. It was this which gave a house the appearance of the initial letter of Queen

Elizabeth's name, though we are always warned by the learned to attach no importance to this coincidence.

Two additional features marked the building, an increase in the number and size of its mullioned windows and a tendency to break up the roof-line with gables. In earlier buildings, the ascent from floor to floor had been made by a winding stair, for which a turret was provided beyond the line of the walls. But now the staircase became a feature of the interior economy of the house, first a square-shaped adaptation of the circular form built in a box-like well, as occurs very prominently in duplicate at Aston Bury, Hertfordshire, then a broad staircase with landings. The old hall which had been open to the rafters was now ceiled over to give accommodation, if not on the first, at any rate on the second floor. The number of "living-rooms" increased and also the number of bedrooms, while towards the end of the period it became *de rigueur* to instal a particular apartment which ran the whole length of the range called the "long gallery," the full reason for which has never been satisfactorily explained.

It is perhaps due to the influence of architectural writers with a strong bias towards later classical work that the Elizabethan house as we see it in the plates of Nash's *Mansions* is perhaps under a cloud of disapproval, slight or severe. It is a matter of individual taste, but some feel that the Elizabethan Manor House, with its symmetrical front of gables above many extensive ranges of mullioned windows, is one of the finest characteristic productions of the time, and indeed of the English genius. It has been pointed out that the mixture of motives in the architecture is paralleled by the jumble of sources from which much of the literature, such as Spenser's *Faerie Queen*, is composed, and it is interesting to observe that far more of the houses of this style are either owned by the National Trust, or are otherwise accessible to the public, than of any other period. Many of the objections which are urged against the Elizabethan Manor are due to the enormous scale and the vast size on which some of the largest were erected, such as Burghley and Hatfield. Knole at Sevenoaks* in its fine park is one of these great town-like piles, a veritable treasure house of contemporary and later furniture, silver and needlework. One reason for the pretentious over-elaboration sometimes found may be due in the additions due to to Victorian decorators.

In a number of cases this grandiose scale has led to the pulling down of vast ranges of apartments which later owners felt themselves unable to maintain. At Audley End no less than two courtyard ranges have disappeared, though their appearance is preserved for us in Winstanley's *Engravings*, just as we can see the splendours of the Bucks Hall at Cowdray,* the non-symmetrical Tudor house ruined by fire at the end of the eighteenth century, in S. H. Grimm's drawings in the British Museum.

The smaller sixteenth-century manor house can be quite pleasant and unpretentious, as at Swanbourne and Marsh Gibbon in Buckinghamshire, but by a curious turn of fortune there are not many of these giving access to the public. Fountains Hall* is a good stone example of moderate size, and Fawley Court, Herefordshire, is a farm-house, as is also that fine example of English timber crafts-manship, The Ley, Weobley Marsh. But farmhouse interiors have usually been subjected to deteriorating alteration, which has diminished or obliterated much of their original fine character. Symmetrical design had been reached in some cases before the incorporating of Renais-sance features, as at Eastbury House, Barking,* now pre-served, Hengrave in Suffolk (107), and Burlington Court, Somerset, though in the latter case its long tenancy as a farmhouse has caused its complete interior reconstruction. If Wollaton* is of huge and burly bulk, and Longford Castle* has the weird layout of three towers arranged as a triangle with connecting ranges, little objection can be taken to the fine, simple design of such a house as Monta-cute,* by Sir Edward Phelips, 1585, which incorporates in one front a porch transported from an earlier house at Clifton Maybank, and still preserves its charming garden layout.

Hardwick Hall* is outstanding for its immense ranges of

mullioned windows; in fact, Astley, which has continuous window ranges, has been hailed as the first example of the modern inclination towards unlimited light and air. Hardwick is also noteworthy for its great coloured plaster hunting frieze. Aston Hall,* a museum of the city of Birmingham, is almost contemporary with Inigo Jones' Palace at Whitehall (v. below). It preserves its gatehouse and a great staircase of typical interest, as well as a long gallery, and also exemplifies the shrinking of the great hall to an entrance chamber. East Riddlesden,* also accessible to the public, is typical of a whole range of houses in the well-defined low-browed northern version of the Elizabethan vernacular. Another great house with fine gardens which will shortly be made accessible to the public is Blickling Hall, Norfolk, known for its connection with the Boleyns, bequeathed to the National Trust by the late Lord Lothian.

"Wilderhope of the Smallmans," a great four-square stone building with a circular wooden staircase in the remote recesses of Wenlock Edge, has now become a youth hostel, and will therefore be cared for after a period of neglect. But it is impossible to speak of many other fine halls such (e.g.) as Levens* and Sizergh in Westmorland. Chastleton, in Oxfordshire,* is a great (e.g.) four-square stone house of the early seventeenth century, unpretentious if a little solid and massive. One of its rooms shows the early Renaissance interior at its best, with its wood panelling and pendented ceiling. It may be compared with the magnificent room at Gilling Castle, with Bernard *Dininck-hoff's* fine painted glass and the equally elaborate interior, with inlaid panelling, from Sizergh Castle, Westmorland, which now can be seen at the Victoria and Albert Museum.*

The destruction rained from the skies has wiped out the centre of Coventry, but only fragments of the glorious mediaeval city remained, as may be seen from the published selection of Troughton's drawings, a unique and invaluable record, which have fortunately survived the destruction of St. Mary's Hall, where they had usually been stored. The Hunnish demolition by fire and explosion is only the culmination of a long period of destruction throughout the

111   A typical Jacobean ceiling, Boston House, Brentford

110   Church Lane, Ledbury, Herefordshire

112 Kew Palace, a red brick building of the mid-seventeenth century

113 A small house of the later eighteenth century, Chesham, Buckinghamshire

eighteenth and especially the nineteenth centuries. To take ornate timber houses, St. Peter's Lodge, Bristol has succumbed to the aerial attack on the city, but the earlier loss of Park Hall, Oswestry, is due to the too common misfortune of a twentieth-century fire, and the interesting house of Lynmore, Montgomery, with its decorative stair, was just torn down after the first Great War.

LATER JACOBEAN, STUART AND PALLADIAN

Shortly after the arrival of James I there came that fourth impulse mentioned a little while back, in the shape of a reformation in the Italianate idea, a determined attempt to make the English house look really and truly like the classical buildings that were being erected on the Continent. Inigo Jones was almost the first person to go and study the the question on the spot, and when the old Royal Banqueting House at Whitehall was burned down Jones replaced it by one in pure classic design (finished 1622). This, of course, was a hall and not a house, but his ideas of what a house in the exact classic manner should be may be studied in the Queen's House at Greenwich* which he built about the same time, though it was not finished until 1635.

The new development was cut short by the clash of the Civil War, and no great buildings were put up between 1642 and the Restoration in 1660. Meanwhile the genius of Inigo Jones was allowed to waste away.

The exuberance which prevailed under the restored monarchy encouraged another outburst of building and a second outstanding genius made his appearance in the shape of Sir Christopher Wren. He also went abroad to study the Continental interpretation of classicism, and though he did not reach the fountain-head in Italy he was able to inspect the works of one of the most important Renaissance buildings then in progress of erection, namely the Louvre Palace. His fame, like that of Jones, rests on his power to adapt the classical forms to an English setting. And the influence of both these masters in rationalising a pagan manner, devised for a sunny climate, into forms adapted for a tepid Christian protestantism (at home and in church) in a comparatively chilly land remained paramount right down to the middle of the Victorian era.

When the eighteenth century dawned, the rage for "pure" classical architecture in every sort of building knew no bounds. You had to take thought for your pigstye, as to which of the orders it should be erected in—Doric, Ionic, or Corinthian? The odd thing was that whichever you chose must be carried out in the Roman spirit and not the Greek, although the Greeks were the sole inventors and the only true masters of the classic styles. The craze was all for Roman stuff; Roman emperors must stand in every niche and members of the Greek Pantheon must always be mentioned by their Roman equivalents. The fashionable Grand Tour stopped short of Greece, and even the ruins of Magna Grecia lying as far west as Sicily were unvisited.

The cry was for correct Roman *orders* and for *proportion*. In the rural districts, where the Gothic tradition lingered on in a vestivial form sadly mixed up with Elizabethan and Jacobean "conceits," new buildings which refused to receive the stamp of the orders were regimented into prevailing notions of proportion. The struggles to secure domestic bliss behind pediments and colonnades became as tragic as they were ridiculous until the happy compromise of the Georgian house was struck.

In the midst of this astonishing craze one new and blessed element of house-construction appeared which had been unknown in the mediaeval hall-house and its Elizaebthan successor. That was the invention of the passgae. It was a simple but epoch-making innovation which secured privacy. Hitherto the only method of getting from one end of a house to another was by going through every room or, in certain cases, as in the public inn, by traversing an outbuilt gallery exposed to the elements. Passages and landings enabled rooms to be multiplied in a house of rectangular plan. And this kind of a house was brought to perfection by the use of a hipped roof instead of a gabled one.

114. Christchurch Mansion, Ipswich: a House chiefly of the later XVIIth Century.

From a water-colour by Leonard Squirrell, R.E., R.I.

TRANSITIONAL

To hark back a bit, there is, however, an intriguing group
of houses having features of both early and late Renaissance, to which attaches all the curious attractiveness

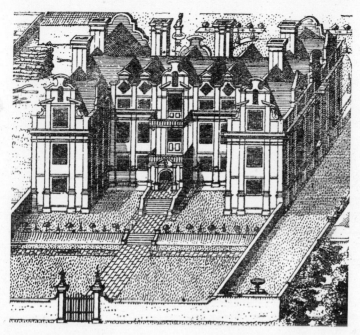

Broome Park, Kent, a house of the mid-seventeenth century
The entrance front as originally designed
[*T. Badeslade, sc. ca. 1720*

characteristic of borderline countries and productions.
Many of them were for long attributed to Inigo Jones, but
modern research has eliminated his connection with most
of them, though one of the few authentic houses of his
design, Raynham, Norfolk, 1636, is not dissimilar in style
to some of these hybrids, but even setting aside the later
remodelling of many of the rooms by William Kent, the
interior is of a far more developed and robust classic type.
The earlier range of Wilton, Wiltshire, is unquestionably

19

from his hand, a well-balanced exterior design with a range
of splendid rich interiors. There is an incongruous neo-
gothic range by James Wyatt. These transitional houses
have usually a close range of gables, often curly and twisted,
possibly due to Dutch influence. Among them may be
mentioned Kew Palace* (112); Swakeley's, Middlesex,*
belonging to the National Trust, and recently used as a
Foreign Office Club, and Broome Park, Kent, which
was painfully pulled about by the late Lord Kitchener
whose motto *Thorough* was direful in its results. The place
was in danger of being pulled down, when it was opened as
an hotel, but we have not ascertained its present fate. The
great White Hart Inn at Scole* on the main Norwich Road
is an effective building of this type in brick, built during the
Commonwealth. Its tremendous beam sign of allegorical
elaboration unfortunately vanished during the nineteenth
century. It will be seen that Kew Palace, with its symmetrical design and sash windows is definitely late Renaissance
in trend, though curiously enough the interiors had an early
Jacobean flavour. The same may be said of the staircase
at Scole. The later work at Forde Abbey* might also be
included in this category, and the interiors here are of
curious awkward transitional design, while the ceilings have
the highly modelled bands characteristic of the Carolean
period, but lacking in its usual repose. The staircase is one
of those imposing rolling scroll designs found in the latter
part of the seventeenth century. At Lees Court, Kent, an
interesting house unfortunately burnt some years ago, there
were some Louis XIII chimney-pieces reminiscent of
Barbier's designs, as may be found among Inigo Jones' own
designs.

In such buildings as Quebec House, Westerham,* and
Christchurch Mansion, Ipswich,* (114), which houses a
museum of the City of Ipswich, the later Renaissance has
taken full possession, and only the slightly insouciant shape
of such features as the gable remains as a trace of the earlier
manner.

115   The Earl of Burlington's Villa, Chiswick, a century ago

From a watercolour by John Buckler

116, 117 Kedleston, Derbyshire. Designed by Robert Adam.

The Park and Entrance Fronts

LATE RENAISSANCE

The Late Renaissance may be claimed as a definite style which flourished from the Restoration to the death of Queen Anne. As we have seen, it is usual to attribute the domestic style then evolved to the influence of Sir Christopher Wren, though apart from Hampton Court, little actual house architecture can be attributed to his personal hand. It is really an unpretentious vernacular interlude between the more Italianate design of Inigo Jones and Webb and the early Georgian Palladianism, for to whom the eighteenth-century architects returned with reverent gusto, since Palladio was their Allah and Inigo Jones his prophet. Succeeding Inigo Jones was the curious episode of Vanbrugh, who succeeded in developing a distinctive if heavy Baroque, individual and effective if not carried out on too large a scale, such as at Blenheim. His work is best studied in its smaller manifestations, such as King's Weston, Bath, and a house at Oxford, though perhaps the derelict pile of Seaton Delaval is the most original expression of his genius. The recent destruction of the giant pile of Castle Howard by fire is a real loss to English domestic architecture.

The Late Renaissance house, especially of the medium size and smaller type, continued right through the eighteenth century, and many of this type remain on the outskirts of country towns (113) and in small parks, the produce of anonymous builders who succeeded in thus evolving the second markedly vernacular style of house building, following after over a century's interval on the Tudor. The comfortable little red-brick house with its well-proportioned doorway, white sashed windows and possibly glazed cupola, is as unpretentious as it is effective, standing sometimes right up to the village street, but more often behind its little drive, with well-proportioned open ironwork screen or a sweep of posts and chains. It is only needful to think of the number of houses in Salisbury Close, of the late examples in quiet Stamford streets, of Groombridge Place and of the Mote House, Downton, to realise that the productions of this period have much to commend them to us, and little to which even purists can take exception. Some of the larger late Renaissance houses, however, such as Melton Constable, Norfolk, and Denham Place, are not only excellent in their proportions but are repositories of fine craftsmanship. Chatsworth,* by William Talman, contemporary and rival of Wren, replaced an earlier house in the last years of the seventeenth century. It is an excellent successful design and shows what a finely worked out production could be made for a great estate owner. It is a matter for congratulation that the public can view and appreciate its grand lay-out, splendid suite of interiors and fine carving. Petworth* is equally splendid in its carving and paintings, but the design is definitely French by an unknown architect; Boughton, Northamptonshire, is the only other parallel Gothic example. The interiors of this style are wood panelled, occasionally with carving finely architectural or in the elaborate design of the Naturalistic school, called after Grinling Gibbons. At this period modelled plasterwork entered on a new and luxuriant phase. It is preferable to call it "high relief" rather than with Bankart "Naturalistic." Though its period of flourishing was brief, its productions are numerous, and occasionally a plain or austere exterior will conceal a series of suave and gracious interiors, with fine ceilings, as at Eye Manor, Herefordshire.

THE PALLADIAN HOUSE

Let it be admitted that the great Palladian house, already touched on (p. 136), was more often than not cold, pretentious, and inconveniently arranged for human habitation. It is well to remember that it was frequently a repository for furniture, plate, paintings, and pottery of refinement unsurpassed in the English centuries. It is curious that although the design books of the Palladian architects— Gibbs, Kent, and the rest—swarm with designs for smaller country houses, these do not seem in many cases to have been built; a pity, when one considers how successful are the comparatively few small to medium places of the mid-eighteenth century which have come down to us. It is only possible to give even mention of a few, such as Marlow Place, Wolterton, Norfolk, and Boreham House, Essex, now an agricultural research station. Bath is full of dignified manifestations of the Palladian house, single, paired, or grouped into series. We illustrate the Earl of Burlington's villa at Chiswick* (115) which, after a period of use as a lunatic asylum, is now in the hands of the Chiswick local authorities. One wonders, however, if anything will ever be done to mitigate its desolate forlornness. It must be remembered that some of the larger houses of the mid-eighteenth century were, when carried out by eminent architects for owners with unlimited wealth at their disposal, filled with decoration of splendid craftsmanship. It is only necessary to instance Houghton Hall for the Walpoles and Holkham* for the Cokes.

LATER STYLES IN REVIVED CLASSIC

The coterie of Palladian architects—Kent, Leoni, Gibbs, Ware, Flitcroft, and their fellows—did not after all have a very long innings, though they had for a time completely in their hands the carrying out of all important works. The first steps of a movement which ended in consistent and literal reproduction of Greek classic forms was taken by Robert Adam and his brothers some little time before the middle of the eighteenth century. In actual fact the exterior design of an Adam house is little different in most cases from the Palladian; some people indeed call them usually dull, but in the interior, to the annoyance of traditionalists of the type of Sir William Chambers, a new style of design was evolved by the introduction of a composite collection of motives, partly acquired on the brothers' travels, or obtained from Roman stucco work and Pompeiian sources. In gradually fining down the stock Palladian forms of door and chimneypiece with which they started, they aimed at, and obtained, a much lighter effect with an access of grace and delicacy. The ceiling was patterned in light arabesques interspersed with small lunettes or panels of paintings of classic subjects, frequently carried out by such artists as

Biagio Rebecca and Angelica Kauffmann (118). The brothers specialised in designing even the door and lighting fittings and sometimes also the table appointments. In their larger houses, such as Kedleston,* here illustrated (116–118), they could still incorporate vast monumental halls suitable for national assemblies, but their tendency generally was towards lightness, and by such features as curved ends of rooms they worked for that "Movement" which was one of their favourite aims. In addition to Kedleston, a smaller Adam house accessible to the public is Kenwood, Highgate,* thanks to a Guinness bequest, with a collection of eighteenth-century pictures. The Adams left behind them a large quantity of work, much of which still survives, though a good deal of their town work, such as Harewood House, Hanover Square, has vanished. It is most unfortunate that Lansdowne House and 20, St. James' Square, have recently been added to the list of regrettable disappearances. Perhaps one of the most characteristic and refined town houses is 20, Portman Square, the home of the Courtauld Institute, to which, if it survives aerial bombardment, as a discreet interested visitor, you would probably not be unwelcome.

Frequently the Adams added to or reconstructed earlier houses; occasionally, indeed, the brothers would work on houses begun by Palladian architects, such as James Paine (as at Kedleston) and Carr of York, who themselves would work separately on one individual mansion. It is not possible to give particulars of these, though it is extremely interesting to work out the course of events. Then again, Wyatt would occasionally carry further an interior decoration of an Adam house, as at Heveningham, Suffolk, and Adam houses have also received additions or have been partially reconstructed by nineteenth-century architects, such as Sir Charles Barry at Bowood. A house of this category is Harewood House, Yorkshire,* which contains some extremely characteristic work by Adam, especially the great gallery, and has a fine collection of specially made furniture by Chippendale, of which the original accounts are preserved. It is fortunate for the public that this house is in the list of "accessibles."

118 The Dining-room, Kedleston

119 Bedford Square and Gower Street, Bloomsbury

120 Royal York Crescent, Clifton

121 A neo-Grec. villa, Cheltenham

REGENCY ARCHITECTURE IN THE WEST

The Adam style of interior decoration was carried on by such designers as James Wyatt, some of whose work, as at Crichel, Dorset, is of extreme and effective refinement. Henry Holland also worked in a similar manner, and it is a matter for regret that Carlton Palace had disappeared, though its rooms can still be seen in the coloured aquatints of Pyne's *Royal Residences*; his works at Apthorpe* may be visited. Thomas Leverton also produced some charming town houses, of which No. 1, Bedford Square is an outstanding example. It is unfortunate there are not many houses of this particular type open to the public, but Heaton Park, Manchester,* a museum of the City Corporation, is a typical example and well worth a visit. The destruction by bombing of Wyatt's Trinity House near the Tower, is a lamentable disaster, as it possessed a complete range of excellent contemporary fittings and furniture,[1] all of which have been destroyed. James (Athenian) Stuart had a limited output, but his interiors in the house at 15, St. James' Square, now a professional institution, are extremely rich in design.

THE REGENCY STYLE

The stage was set for the distinctive and delicate style which is called "Regency," with its literal recapitulation of Greek motives, especially the Anthenion. It is a style of refined restraint with stucco as standard finishing which is just beginning to have justice done to it in the way of exploration, appreciation, and understanding, as the exigencies of modern urban development are tearing it from us. In this style stucco villas appear in Regent's Park and at Cheltenham, in a few parts of London and much of Brighton. John Nash bore a hand in a more robust Roman version and (e.g.) his Cornwall Terrace, Regent's Park is an outstanding and vigorous production, though it is doubtful how long most of such work will be spared. The former St. Pancras Vicarage, by Inwood, was a charming little house recently swept away, and a few villas still remain at

[1] v. Jourdain's *English Decoration and Furniture of the Later Eighteenth Century* (The Library of Decorative Art).

Highbury and Kennington, though they are a doomed and dwindling race.

The most original architect of the Regency period is Sir John Soane, and both exteriors and interiors of Pitshanger Manor, Ealing* show his characteristic style, in which he intentionally abstained from the interior use of the orders. It is open to inspection, as the house is now one of the Ealing Public Libraries. Sir John's own house in Lincoln's Inn Fields,[1] if we do not pay much attention to its somewhat freakish exterior, has a good series of interiors which show the setting of an early nineteenth-century dilettante collector. A characteristic smaller type of country house, by Soane, is Moggerhanger, Bedfordshire, which, as it is now a sanatorium, may possibly be open to inspection on judicious application. Tyringham, Buckinghamshire, is another of his works, to which a later dome has been added. Other Regency architects are Smirke, Ferguson and Foulston, who was active in the Plymouth district, and Papworth at Cheltenham, where the effect of a Regency lay-out of villas and terraces can be well studied and enjoyed. These houses have a number of railings and balconies in an individual local light form of ironwork which is more reminiscent of the productions of a century earlier than the heavier cast-iron contemporary work. Trellis-work, verandahs, and balconies in the Regency style are one of its outstanding attractions, as well as shallow segmental bays, singly or in series which in the interior give an effect of subtle refinement to the ends of rooms. If the classic ornamentation of these rooms does not make a very outstanding show, contemporary designs can be seen in more diversified richness in the design books of the period, particularly Ackermann's *Repository*. Thomas Hope has left a series of Greek interiors in his published work, and the idealised Regency interior with contemporary furniture and appropriate Greek costume is well seen in the charming engravings of Henry Moses' *Modern Costume* (1823).

Before the classic tradition had faded away, houses of Neo-Gothic type had already begun to be erected, and so

[1] Now a Museum open at certain times, and generally on discreet application.

accomplished a revived classic designer as James Wyatt
produced the great pile of Ashridge, now the Bonar Law

The Morning Room, Sir John Soane's House,
Lincoln's Inn Fields

[*W. Curtis Green, R.A. del*

Training Institute for young Conservatives. Of these
curious productions Knebworth,* Donnington Hall,* famed
for its use as a German officers' prison camp in the last war,

Bayons' Hall, Lincolnshire,* and Alton Towers, Stafford-shire,* are open to public inspection. The latter, with its fine gardens, is a remodelling by the younger Prigin of an earlier Gothic house. The tale of houses open to the public may be rounded off with the Italianate pile of Queen Victoria's Osborne House* in the Isle of Wight.

GARDENS

There was one other thing which helped materially to make the Georgian country house the "desirable residence" that we know it to be and that was the development of the art of landscape gardening. Artificial as this was, to begin with, and something of an insult to the scenic pride of Nature, it made a man think about the site of a house before he built it. It made him choose an aspect and a view, and it made him so combine these amenities that the house would look well placed from any point at which the public gaze might rest on it. We owe not only the settings of our "stately homes" of the eighteenth century to the persuasive powers of the landscape gardeners but also those park lands in which they stand, where the best oaks have been left standing in isolation, and great clumps of trees (now so old as to look natural) have been sited as unerringly as the house.

The cult of landscape gardening supplies perhaps one of the most outstanding examples of a fashion originating in England spreading very extensively and with much thoroughness, to the whole of the more civilised parts of the continent of Europe. *Le Jardin Anglais* had in its day a vogue which almost equalled that of French decoration. On the other hand, when pushed to extremes, exception was taken to the gaunt and monotonous results by which a bare tree-dotted field stretched without a break right up to the doors of the houses (116, 117). It was pointed out that this fashion, though called "gardening" and resulting in a fine park, made no provision for flowers, which were occasionally, like poor relations, allotted a small space by the kitchen garden. In addition the advocates of a more architectural lay-out maintained that this so-called following of nature was in itself artificial, and that the house was definitely a human non-natural architectural feature, and needed something of a more regular design in the way of its immediate surroundings, which could gradually become less formal, and lead, by a carefully graded transition, to the park. In the Tudor era and throughout the seventeenth century, gardens of course were in the greatest possible contrast to the later landscape productions, and were entirely formal, with forecourts, terraces, "mounts," geometrical beds, topiary even, regular pieces of water, and avenues. The whole garden controversy, which lasted for the best part of a century, is fascinating and amusing to review. Scorn was poured out in lampoons by contemporary writers upon the ridiculous excesses of the formality from which William Kent started the breakaway; the blank dullness of the extreme landscape school was later in its turn castigated among others by Sir William Chambers and Richard Payne Knight. Nowadays we are able to gauge impartially something of the merits of these contrasting and conflicting styles, and can appreciate the pleasant lay-out of Montacute, the grace and dignity of Drayton House, Northamptonshire, the topiary figures of Levens and Chastleton, as well as the water-gardens of Westbury-on-Severn, Gloucestershire, and the remains of the canals at Wrest, Bedfordshire. Stow House, Buckinghamshire, and Castle Howard, of the landscape school, show the amusing tendency which persisted well into the landscape period, to dot the ground with temples, mausoleums, summer-houses, statues, obelisks, bridges and the like. The Adam house of Croome Court, Worcestershire, is also outstanding for this treatment. It is one of the typical works of Lancelot or "Capability" Brown, the high priest of the extreme landscape style who destroyed many fine gardens, and whose methods of work were modified in the direction of a less extreme result by Humphrey Repton in the early nineteenth century. Many country houses, feeling the bare effect of the landscape park and simple provided themselves in the nineteenth century with a formal garden on a smaller or larger scale, as at Holkham,* Norfolk; in fact Blenheim has only recently completed its lay-out on these lines. The latter part of the nineteenth century witnessed a return to the use of massed flowers, the scheming of coloured borders on a systematic basis, a revival sponsored by William Robinson and Gertrude Jekyll. This was followed very soon by a revival of the formal garden under the influence of a school of architects. The apotheosis of the formal garden at the commencement of the eighteenth century can be seen by turning the plates of Kip's *Nouveau Théâtre de la Grande Bretagne*, and there was much that was imposing and dignified, even if occasionally artificial, in these elaborate lay-outs with their numbers of smaller enclosures and avenues stretching far over the landscape.

The custom has spread very widely of permitting the public to view many famous gardens in most of the counties of England on one or two stated days of the year on payment of a small fee, the proceeds being devoted to the local nursing association. The majority of the great English gardens are thus open to the public at the time of their greatest beauty; many parks are accessible throughout the year, through the good nature of the landowners or by the preservation of rights of way across them. In wartime many of these gardens are closed, but some are still available. Local announcements should be followed and inquiries made.

Thus we come to the end of the great pre-Servant-Problem days which began to crumble when the Industrial Revolution set in and finally went to pieces after the invention of the cinematograph.

Index

(The references in heavier type are to the *figure numbers* of the illustrations)

Ev a